Theodore Roosevelt

and the

Politics of Power

The Library of American Biography

EDITED BY OSCAR HANDLIN

Withdrawn by
Whitman College Library

G. Wallace Chessman

Theodore Roosevelt
and the
Politics of Power

Edited by Oscar Handlin

PENROSE MEMORIAL LIBRARY WHITMAN COLLEGE

Little, Brown and Company • *Boston*

COPYRIGHT © 1969, BY G. WALLACE CHESSMAN

ALL RIGHTS RESERVED. NO PART OF THIS BOOK MAY BE REPRODUCED IN ANY FORM OR BY ANY ELECTRONIC OR MECHANICAL MEANS INCLUDING INFORMATION STORAGE AND RETRIEVAL SYSTEMS WITHOUT PERMISSION IN WRITING FROM THE PUBLISHER, EXCEPT BY A REVIEWER WHO MAY QUOTE BRIEF PASSAGES IN A REVIEW.

LIBRARY OF CONGRESS CATALOG CARD NO. 68-20501

A

E
757
.C55

Published simultaneously in Canada
by Little, Brown & Company (Canada) Limited

PRINTED IN THE UNITED STATES OF AMERICA

To the memory of my parents

Editor's Preface

IT WAS appropriate that Theodore Roosevelt should have entered the White House, just as the twentieth century opened. He was the first modern chief executive of the United States.

For thirty-five years, since the death of Lincoln, the nation had suffered from the atrophy of presidential power. A succession of weak men had proved incapable of dealing seriously with the novel problems and responsibilities created by industrialization within the country and by imperialism in the world outside its boundaries. The weakness of these presidents deepened the difficulties created by the slowness of the federal government to assume a role commensurate with the new problems.

Roosevelt was uniquely qualified by training and personality to reverse the trend. His patrician background, his education, and his grasp of the national and international situations set him apart from the men whom he succeeded in Washington. His vigorous, colorful, forceful personality attracted widespread public attention and deep affection. As a result, he was able to face up to the problems that his predecessors had avoided. In some matters, labor and conservation for instance, he established fruitful precedents. In others, diplomacy for instance, he made false starts. But in any case, he illuminated the questions with which his successors would have to deal. He therefore stood at a strategic point in the emergence of modern America. His career thus throws light on the problems of transition of the nation from the nineteenth to the twentieth century.

OSCAR HANDLIN

Contents

Contents

Theodore Roosevelt

and the

Politics of Power

I

"I'll Make My Body"

1858-1880

IT WAS the first day he had spent at the White House. His wife Edith was still at Oyster Bay, making final arrangements for the move to Washington, so the new President had asked his two sisters and their husbands to dine with him. Now at table he reminded Bye and Corinne that this was their father's birthday.

"I have realized it as I signed papers all day long, and I feel that it is a good omen that I begin my duties in this house on this day," Theodore remarked. "I feel as if my father's hand were on my shoulder, and as if there were a special blessing over the life I am to lead here."

Just then the coffee was being passed, and with it a little boutonniere to each gentleman. The flower given to the President was a yellow saffronia rose. "Is it not strange!" Roosevelt exclaimed. "This is the rose we all connect with my father."

His sisters agreed. The elder Theodore, Corinne recalled, had pruned the saffronia roses with special care; "he always picked one for his buttonhole from that bush, and whenever we gave him a rose, we gave him one of those."

The President turned even more serious. "I think," he concluded, "there is a blessing connected with this."

It would have been remarkable if the memory of their father had not touched these three that night in 1901. Though he had died over twenty-three years before, at the age of 46, he had influenced his children more than most men do. His boundless energy, his keen interest in life's every aspect, his dedicated devotion to his many responsibilities, all had affected his progeny. Enthusiastic yet patient, delightfully gay yet sternly moral, loving yet firm, he had been, in so many ways, the ideal father. In particular he had given of himself to his first son, the asthmatic, feeble little Teedie. The molding of that boy into a man had been a father's task.

Theodore Roosevelt Senior came of substantial stock. In America his lineage went back to Claes Martenszen Van Roosevelt, a farmer and member of the Dutch Reformed Church, who had arrived at New Amsterdam in 1649. The line had passed through five generations of traders and merchants to Cornelius Van Schaak Roosevelt, who in 1840 had become head of Roosevelt and Kobbe, a family hardware firm founded after the American Revolution. Under Cornelius' direction the company had prospered in the importing of plate glass; at the same time, as a founder and one of the original directors of the Chemical National Bank, he had moved the Roosevelt interests into a field that would better weather the depression of the 1870's. Father of five sons by his wife Margaret Barnhill, a Philadelphian of English and Quaker descent and the only non-Dutch member of the family, Cornelius ruled a comfortable domain from his mansion overlooking Union Square. Son Theodore, though too light-hearted by burgher standards, would carry on the tradition.

For his own bride Theodore had gone farther south, to Georgia. There, at nineteen years of age, he had met the beautiful Martha Stewart Bullock, daughter of a line of planters, lawyers, and statesmen that went back to the James Bullock who crossed from Glasgow to Charleston in 1729. And in 1853, after a three-year courtship conducted mainly through letters, "Thee" had married the nineteen-year-old "Mittie" and brought her back to New York. They had moved into a new row house, a four-story brownstone at 33 (later 28) East 20th Street, next door to his brother Robert Barnwell Roosevelt, and only a few blocks up Broadway from his father's.

It was a strange world for a Southern girl. The businesslike bustle of the city contrasted sharply with the rural life of Georgia. More difficult still were the family dinners every Sunday noon at father Cornelius Roosevelt's, where by tradition Dutch was spoken. In the privacy of her own household, in a prized gown in which she dressed so carefully, she could be the gay self Thee found so appealing. But in January 1855 she bore their first child, Anna ("Bamie" or "Bye"). When the infant suf-

fered a spinal injury that caused the family to fear she
would never be able to walk, Mittie must have welcomed
her mother's decision to sell the Georgia plantation and
move north in 1856 with her only unmarried daughter,
Anna, into the growing establishment on East 20th
Street.

Thus on October 27, 1858 the matriarchal Mrs. Bullock was on hand to comfort her daughter in the birth of
a second child, a boy, weighing eight-and-a-half pounds,
and named Theodore for his father. "It is as sweet and
pretty a young baby as I have ever seen," Mrs. Bullock declared; "No chloroform or any such thing was used, no
instruments were necessary, consequently the dear little
thing has no cuts or bruises about it." Mittie thought the
baby "hideous . . . a cross between a terrapin and Dr.
Young," but there was no sign of the sickliness that was
to cloud so many days and nights of his childhood. In
1860 came Elliott, and a year later the second daughter,
Corinne. Thee had just turned thirty, and the great war
of the North and the South was in its sixth month.

These were trying times for the young parents. Bamie,
at least, appeared well on the way to full recovery, aided
by a harness that supported her spine and a father who
encouraged her constantly to exercise. Young Theodore,
though, was pitifully frail and increasingly subject to
severe attacks of asthma. Sometimes at night Thee
would walk the floor for hours with the boy in his arms;
at times he would even take him out in the carriage, to
drive through the silent streets until the seizure subsided
in sleep. "Teedie was very unwell last night," Mittie

wrote her husband in December 1861; "I was up with him six or seven times during the night." "Teedie is too much sick," Thee declared a month later. "It worries me."

The strain was the greater because the glass-importing business frequently took Theodore away to Europe or across the Alleghenies. After the outbreak of the war he was often gone, too, first lobbying for a bill that would enable soldiers to make regular allotments from their pay to their dependents, then serving as one of the three Allotment Commissioners from New York appointed by President Lincoln to carry out the new law in the field. Mittie was glad that at least he was not fighting; she couldn't have borne that, not with two of her brothers in the Confederate Navy and her own sympathies so firmly on the Southern side. Thee, influenced in part perhaps by his Quaker background, had decided not to enlist. That decision would rankle later in a militant son's breast, but the father pursued his course without outward excuse or recrimination. His contribution to the war effort was at a personal sacrifice to him and his wife and his young children on East 20th Street. All suffered, each in his way.

The tension among the "big people" was not without its effects upon the children. Teedie may not have known how it pained his mother to see him marching about in his Zouave shirt, yet in resentment at maternal discipline he once prayed Divine Providence to "grind the Southern troops to powder." Bamie vividly recalled how the three Southern women busily packed mysterious parcels to take on picnics with the children in the park, when Thee was away, for transfer to those who would run the blockade.

Whatever the true effects of such tension, and despite illnesses and petty jealousies, the young Roosevelts were a lively, mischievous flock, lovingly shepherded by Aunt Annie and the servants. After 1862 there was welcome release in the summer, at a country place in Madison, New Jersey, where the children could roam freely at their games, "always responsive to some story of Theodore's which seemed to cast a glamour around our environment." In the summer of 1865 their cousins from Georgia joined them; the next year they got their first pony — "Pony Grant." So the nursery years passed with the war.

Young Theodore's character began to come into sharper focus. At play, Mittie's "little berserker" evidenced the extraordinary energy typical of his father, but in periods of seclusion induced by "asmer" attacks and delicate health he was becoming an omnivorous reader. Tales of adventure and articles on natural history especially attracted him; he discovered both, with a generous mixture of moral lessons and kind-hearted sentiments, in the magazine *Our Young Folks,* which he much later asserted "taught me more than any text book." The sight of a dead seal in a Broadway market further stimulated his imagination; he recorded its measurements with a care that became habitual, began at once to write a natural history, and was soon collecting specimens for the "Roosevelt Museum of Natural History" in a bookcase upstairs. By 1867 he was keeping live mice in his room, by the spring of 1868 he was writing his mother in Georgia that "I jumped with delight when I found you heard the mocking-bird, get some of its feathers if you can." "Wont you drive Mamma to some battlefield," he asked his father at the same time, "for she is going to get me some trophies."

The lure of the outdoors had his father's assistance. The illnesses that afflicted Teedie and Connie had convinced Theodore that their windowless middle room was unhealthful and useless, so he had the back bedroom overlooking the garden converted into an open-air piazza where they might play all year long. In summer he packed the family off to the country, to Madison first and then to Barrytown in Dutchess County. On August 10, 1868 at Barrytown, Theodore, Jr. recorded "an attack of the asmer" in his new diary, but later pages catalogued a good deal of riding, walking, and swimming. "I took a ride of *six* miles on pony grant, before breakfast up to Crugers Island," the boy noted on August 18. Two days later, after repeating that feat, he declared "I will always have a ride of six miles before breakfast now."

That winter of 1868-69 the father planned a family trip to Europe. His business was prospering, and his wife particularly wanted to visit her brothers exiled in England. The ones who would benefit most, though, were the children; a real education, he was persuaded, came more easily through travel than through tutor or school. And travel he laid out, beginning in England in May

1869, and proceeding through Scotland, the Low Countries, the Rhine Valley, Switzerland, and northern Italy; then to Vienna and back through Germany to Paris by November; thence south to Italy for the winter, returning to Paris in March, and finally to England and home by the end of May 1870. With four children ranging from eight to fourteen years of age, it would truly be a Grand Tour.

In the retrospect of autobiography the younger Theodore did not have much good to say of this epic journey; his letters and diaries of the time tell a different story. His reactions to the sights and events, as recorded with care (and sometimes style) in his journal, reveal an observant nature. The glimpses of him poring over his geography book, or listening to his father read *Lady of the Lake* as they walked through the Trossachs, or exploring the ruins of Pompeii and the heights of Vesuvius, disclose education in a true sense. There was a broadening of perspective, though the consciousness of being "different" probably contributed to his later emphasis upon being "an American." If he much later recalled "cordially hating" the trip and regarding Europe "with the most ignorant chauvinism and contempt," it may have been in part because upset stomachs and asthma persistently troubled him in hotel after hotel. Through much of that year abroad his existence had the paradoxical pattern of vigorous sight-seeing by day and painful illness at night.

Being a determined man, and believing that an outdoor life and frequent changes of air would in time work their medicine, the elder Theodore had refused to coddle his son. But before another winter set in, after the return to the States, he decided that more drastic measures were necessary. "You have the mind," he told the thin-legged eleven-year-old, "but you have not the body, and without the help of the body, the mind cannot go as far as it should." Then he threw down the challenge. "You must *make* your body," the father declared. "It is hard drudgery to make one's body, but I know you will do it." Then, as Corinne remembered her mother's story, the frail boy threw back his shoulders, set his jaw, and replied: *"I'll make my body."*

Father and son, each had an intense energy; they also had strong wills. Through that long winter Mittie took the youngster regularly to Wood's Gymnasium for workouts on the bars and the chest-weights machine. Pleased with the progress, Theodore Senior installed similar equipment on the open-air piazza, so that the exercises might continue at home. By summer the regimen was apparently working; there was not a reference to asthma in the diaries of an active month spent in the Adirondacks and the White Mountains. But the succeeding July there was another asthma attack, and it was thought best to send him off to Moosehead Lake in Maine for a "change of air." An encounter with two bullies there, without his younger but more robust brother to defend him, showed how far he still had to go. When he returned home, in the fall of 1872, boxing became a part of the gymnastics.

The mind had its share in harmonious growth. Teedie's health had never been such that he could go to ordinary school, but in that day informal instruction at home was considered quite adequate. At their summer place at Dobbs Ferry in 1872, as "T.D." wrote the Aunt Annie who had watched over their nursery school, "I study English, French, German and Latin now." He was also pursuing nature study methodically; that summer he acquired his first gun, a breech-loading, pin-fire double-barrel of French manufacture, and that fall he went around of his own accord to a "musty little shop" for lessons in taxidermy. For the boy, as for the father, life was a whole: in the great outdoors one found health, sport, and education. And for the father the complete teacher was travel: in the fall of 1872 the whole family embarked upon another yearlong expedition that would take them this time as far east as Egypt and the Holy Land.

For a boy just turned fourteen, a boy who had just put on his first pair of glasses ("I had no idea how beautiful the world was," he would write later, "until I got those spectacles"), it was truly a great adventure. For two months, as they voyaged 538 miles up the Nile, and back again to Cairo, he rode (or rowed) along the bank hunting almost every day, visited the Temple at Karnak and other monuments, worked away at lessons in French and English under Bamie's tutelage. He went through the Suez Canal with his father and Elliott, and then the family journeyed mostly by caravan through Palestine and Syria; young Theodore rode horseback, slept in tents, chased jackals, swam in the Jordan, watched dancing girls. At Beirut they took ship to Athens, and thence to Constantinople, where he jogged along on a horse touring mosque after mosque. By Danube steamer they went to Belgrade, and on to Vienna, where they stayed three weeks while the senior Roosevelt carried out his duties as the American Commissioner to the Exposition there. At last in May there was the night express to Dresden, to the home of Herr Doktor Minkwitz, where Teedie and Elliott would spend five months, chiefly studying German with Fräulein Anna.

Through all this activity Teedie's health remained a concern: several times he suffered from asthma, and at one point in August his mother took him to Switzerland for a change of air. It was apparent, though, that his efforts to "make his body" were producing results. The greater concern of his father was that it was time the boy undertook a more rigorous course of study preparatory to entering Harvard in September 1876. "You cannot imagine how unwillingly I take Theodore, Ellie and Connie from Fräulein and Dresden as the portals of the language commence to open," Mittie wrote. "I wish we had the courage to leave the boys, and what I most wish is that you could come out and they might study all winter." Thee saw the need for a more balanced program: his son was well advanced in natural history and German and English literature, but college would demand much more in classical languages, mathematics, and even English fundamentals. In November 1873 the Roosevelts headed home, to the new house (with a new gymnasium) built in their absence at 6 West 57th Street, close by Central Park. Soon Theodore, Jr. was installed in a rigorous schedule of study and exercise with a private tutor, Arthur H. Cutler, later founder of the Cutler School for Boys in New York.

It was more obvious now that the lines of development led away from his mother. Her warm love had sustained him through trying years; her wit and gaiety still enlivened their times together. But as the family's activities broadened and intensified, Mittie retreated more often to her room. It was said that her health was delicate, and likely she welcomed an excuse to get away. Somehow she had kept up before, but the pace was getting too much for one accustomed to more leisurely Southern ways. Increasingly she showed a passion for cleanliness, an incompetence at money matters and housekeeping, a disposition to be always late for appointments. When she appeared at parties, so immaculately groomed in her beautiful gowns, she impressed all with her charm, but she just couldn't manage life efficiently. To keep up with the Roosevelts, it was not enough just to have energy.

Her convivial husband was of another sort. From the wells of his being he drew such bubbling energy that to the last year of his life he could say "I never seem to get tired." From a disciplined sense of obligation he found the will to direct that energy constructively. So diverse were the ways he expressed himself, so integrated was the pattern, so good-humored did he remain, that only a great efficiency sustained him. Essentially a man of action, he embraced life in all its variety, "seizing the moment" always to enhance experience, concentrating upon each task and opportunity as it arose. In Theodore's activity, everything had its place.

His business affairs had an important part in his life, yet he never allowed money-making to absorb his attention. "You have been perfectly lovely to me in your care of me always," Mittie once wrote him, "and so good and indulgent and thoughtful." With the children, he was "the perfect life of all our enjoyments," young Theodore asserted; "in some unique way," said Corinne, their father "seemed to have the power of responding to the need of each, and we all craved him as our most desired companion." Friends such as John Hay, Joseph H. Choate, and William E. Dodge often called at the Roosevelt home; with Mittie, Thee vastly enjoyed a busy social life of parties and dancing. Sundays he taught Sunday school and attended the Presbyterian church; Sunday evenings he went around to the Newsboys' Lodging House, sometimes to give talks on "patriotism, good citizenship and manly morality." And on Saturdays, often in company with one of his children, he visited other philanthropic "good works," such as the Children's Aid Society, the Orthopedic Hospital, the Museum of Natural History, and the Metropolitan Museum of Art.

"I never knew anyone who got greater joy out of living than did my father," the younger Theodore was to write in his *Autobiography*, "or anyone who more wholeheartedly performed every duty; and no one whom I have ever met approached his combination of enjoyment of life and performance of duty." Certainly his wife was proud of him, but the example he set could be trying. "I watched you get in the carriage with a great constriction across my chest and suddenly waked up to the loneliness of our position and I thought of your unselfishness," Mittie wrote after a wartime parting. "I wish you were not *so good*. It makes me sad," she added; "I am not so strong-minded, as you know, and I feel so dependent."

Endowed with that same intense energy and strong will of the father, the older son was revealing also a capacity for efficiency. Even as a young child he had concentrated intently upon a book, oblivious to the goings-on around him. As his interest in natural history deepened, he had put his observations carefully into a record. His first diaries had shown a similar drive to discipline his thoughts methodically. By the time he was ready to prepare for college, in 1873, every action seemed to have its purpose, every pursuit its place in an integrated program. Theodore would plunge into his interests so completely, with such seeming abandon, that some already regarded him as "eccentric"; what they missed was that in all the flurry of doing what he wanted, he knew always what he was about. If energy was wasted, it was expendable; he had adequate reserves, under good control.

To control energies through sheer efficiency, though, was not enough: morality, as a curb and as a spur, was vital also. So the elder Theodore believed, and acted. As a Christian and a gentleman, he adhered to a strict code of personal conduct. In a spirit of Christian charity commingled with *noblesse oblige,* he also extended a helping hand to the less fortunate. No man, he thought, ought to expect everything to be done for him; the object of philanthropy, as most agreed, was to help others to help themselves. But that was only to say that in any community, all men have duties. For a man in his station to ignore or evade his responsibilities, the elder Theodore was convinced, would be an affront to true stewardship and honorable tradition.

By instruction and example the father impressed these views upon his son. Their full effect would come later, but one incident at Dresden indicated the direction. Adolescent freedom and exercise had made young Theodore more unruly and rough in his manners that year, but when one Percy Cushion "swore like a trooper and used disreputable language . . . I gave him some pretty strong hints, which he at last took, and we do not see much more of him." Percy was "a failure," Theodore wrote his father, but "we have made the acquaintance of another boy . . . a very nice boy, never swears or uses language that could not be uttered in ladies drawing room, and yet is always ready to box or swim or do any other thing we propose." The young Theodore Roosevelt was beginning to apply his code of behavior to others; an apostle of righteousness was beginning to render judgments.

The belief that one could be "a very nice boy" and still be "always ready to box or swim or do any other thing we propose" disclosed a particular strength of the budding moralist. In a man's world his espousal of a high standard of personal conduct invited ridicule as being sissified or effeminate, but not if he evinced hardihood in physical pursuits. A fellow could have a clean mind *and* a sound body: that was the lesson of *Our Young Folks,* that was the motto of the new Y.M.C.A., that was the example of the elder Theodore. Gym exercises would thus relate to larger purposes. The effort to *"make my body"* would undergird a life devoted to reform. And when carried so far as to approach worship of manly prowess, it would support policies of imperialism and power.

The religious attitude behind such views was decidedly muscular. Influenced by his father and still more by his scientific interests, the young Theodore had developed a skeptical attitude, whether toward "the Bones of Saints (or turkeys) in Italy" or the Wailing Wall in Jerusalem where "many of the women were in earnest, but most of the men were shamming." But though Darwinian theory undercut any literal interpretation of Genesis, and though enlightened people rejected the miraculous about Jesus, the Church retained important functions. A witness to a God whose aid men invoked, it was a principal agent also in the moral discipline of society. The Scriptures contained precepts for virtuous living; the Sunday school trained men for righteous action; the true Christian was a soldier enlisted for the good against the evil in the world. It was entirely in keeping that, through three-and-a-half years at Harvard, Theodore would teach a group of boys at Christ Church, Cambridge, only quitting when "a good deal to my amusement and rather to my disgust I [was] requested to resign my Sunday School Class unless I would join the Episcopalian Church!"

Through the last years of preparation for Harvard, the lines of development toward his father retained their purposeful direction. For eight hours a day in winter, and three in summer, there was study under his tutor's guidance: "the young man never seemed to know what idleness was," Cutler later reported, "and every leisure moment would find the last novel, some English classic or some abstruse book on natural history in his hands." There was strenuous exercise, too, in the home gymnasium or at the family's new summer place at Oyster Bay, close by Cove Neck where young Theodore would one day construct "Sagamore." By the summer of 1875, at close to eighteen years of age, he was 5 feet 8 inches tall and weighed 124 pounds; he was a tense, wiry boy, but asthma seldom bothered him, and he was finding pleasure more and more at parties with other young people.

The young Roosevelts had always had playmates among the children of their parents' friends, but after the second trip to Europe, Mittie organized a dancing class at Dodsworth's ballroom and made a greater social effort. Theodore watched his older sister enter upon a round of parties following her New York debut in January 1874; for himself, he was as happy in the company of boys, but still he enjoyed the carefully planned gatherings at New York and Oyster Bay. Untroubled by any pangs of adolescent love, he discovered some of the pleasures his father had in social life. His "strongest appeal was the unquenchable gaiety which seemed to emanate from his whole personality," Fanny Smith afterwards wrote of young Theodore, as she remembered "dreading to sit next him at any formal dinner lest I become so convulsed with laughter at his whispered sallies as to disgrace myself and be forced to leave the room." "He is such fun," the same girl confided to her diary at Oyster Bay, "the most original boy I ever knew."

With an efficient ease so typical of his father, he worked this social activity into the pattern of sports and study: his main goal was to gain admission to college. In the first round of tests, in July 1875, he passed well in the eight subjects he tried; thereafter there was little doubt that in the fall of 1876 he would register at the nation's oldest educational institution. The choice of Harvard for Theodore clearly reflected his interests: under President Eliot that university was pioneering in the liberalization of the classical curriculum through an elective system that afforded much greater opportunity for training in science. The world of nature had always excited the boy most; if he wanted to go on to become a naturalist, his father was willing to "provide an adequate income for him, but he must make up his mind to forgo many of the additional pleasures that accompany a money-making business." By every indication, during that first winter in Cambridge, his son was ready to forsake such pleasures.

What Cutler called "the alert, vigorous character of young Roosevelt's mind" was manifest at Harvard.

Some students and instructors resented the increasing frequency with which he spoke up in classes; he was "a little bumptious" certainly, but then "the courses in Political Economy were very cold and uninteresting before Roosevelt came," said one boy, and "with his appearance and questionings, things livened up." He did particularly well at natural history, winning an "honorable mention" in that field at graduation, yet his overall record was such that he finished twenty-first in a class of 158 and was elected to Phi Beta Kappa. Among friends of his set, he was distinguished for his intelligence and hard work; in the academic rank of his class, as he told Bamie at the start of his senior year, "only one gentleman stands ahead of me."

At times the old enemy, asthma, kept him awake nights in his second-floor room at 16 Winthrop Street, but he kept up his routine of exercise. Harvardmen of the day walked to classes in an indolent, indifferent fashion; Theodore usually ran. He worked out regularly in the gymnasium, and in the spring of his junior year went as far as the finals for the lightweight boxing championship. The slightness of his build fooled much stronger boys like Richard Welling, who was ready to quit an afternoon's ice-skating at Fresh Pond hours before Theodore ("Isn't it bully!") would head home. The long walks, the miles of rowing in the summer, the seemingly constant effort to push his stamina to the limit found their first culmination in three expeditions into the Maine woods with guide Bill Sewall in 1878 and 1879; in a total of 69 days the two men travelled over a thousand miles, more than half on foot, through practically virgin wilderness. Theodore Roosevelt, confessed Sewall, was "a different fellow to guide from what I have ever seen."

"Take care of your morals first," his father advised him, "then your health, and finally your studies." For young Theodore, morality was not much of a problem. Only once did he go with some classmates to a "girlie show" in Boston, and he customarily passed up the wine and tobacco at their parties. In a social life that grew ever more active, he was pleased to remain "perfectly pure." His schedule always had a place for his Sunday school class, and usually church; he had no time for idle frivolity. And he seemed so sincere that it took the edge off a pride at being moral, just as he turned away resentment of his competitiveness by the obvious way in which he seemed always to enjoy himself.

His associations showed a similar pattern. As a freshman he appeared inordinately conscious of the background of those he met: "I most sincerely wish I knew something about the antecedents of my friends," he confided to Corinne; "On this very account I have avoided being very intimate with the New York fellows." Yet after a number of visits to homes in the vicinity he observed that "I can't help being more and more struck by the fact that if the parents are good and *wise*, the son generally does pretty fairly too, although of course this does not always hold." The circle into which he moved in Cambridge and Boston was what was called the "high set"; he was a gentleman, he met "the best people," he was elected into the exclusive Porcellian Club. Yet the friendships he formed were natural rather than snobbish; the men he liked had had much the same upbringing, and while "not brilliant," they were, as he said, "plucky, honorable, and rigidly virtuous." The standard he applied was hardly democratic, yet never narrow.

Congenial yet moral, athletic yet bookish, young Theodore concentrated upon his diverse interests with such intensity that many thought him strange. "He danced just as you'd expected him to dance if you knew him," said his future sister-in-law, "he hopped." He was "studious, ambitious, eccentric," asserted another girl, "not the sort to appeal at first." "I wonder whether he is the real thing," noted classmate William Roscoe Thayer, "or only the bundle of eccentricities he appears."

The father he so much resembled was well pleased. At the Christmas break in the sophomore year, he went so far as to tell his son that he had never caused him a moment's pain, that indeed he was the dearest of his children to him. That amounted to a deathbed confidence, for little more than a month later, worn down by a bitter wrangle over the collectorship of the port of New York, and afflicted by an inoperable tumor, the forty-six-year-old Theodore died. The unexpected blow prostrated the son who earlier had written "I do not think there is a fellow in College who has a family that love him as much as you all do me, and I am *sure* that there is no one who has a Father who is also his best and most intimate friend, as you are mine." The memory of the man bolstered Theodore through his grief. It stiffened his resolve to live a life of which his father would have been proud.

And the next fall he found a new object of intense affection in Alice Hathaway Lee, the seventeen-year-old daughter of the George Cabot Lees of Chestnut Hill, a slender, graceful girl whom he met through his classmate Dick Saltonstall. In a junior year in which he distinguished himself in academics and athletics, Theodore took up a most active social life, even stabling a horse in Cambridge so that he could get over to Chestnut Hill more easily. His first proposal of marriage in June 1879 went unaccepted, and there were times that fall that he walked away the night in lovelorn desperation, but at last in January 1880 Alice consented to marry him. "I am so happy that I dare not trust in my own happiness," he wrote in his diary on January 25. "I drove over to the Lees determined to make an end of things at last; it was nearly eight months since I had first proposed to her, and I had been nearly crazy during the past year; and after much pleading my own sweet, pretty darling consented to be my wife." "I am leading the very happiest life a mortal ever led, with my sweet darling," he exulted that spring to his older sister; "it is awfully hard to study."

His engagement confirmed one change long in the making: he would not go on to be a scientist. His first doubts about a scientific career had appeared in October 1878, just before meeting Alice; they had grown as his courtship progressed, until in February 1880, in notifying a fellow naturalist of his betrothal, Theodore confessed that he had "made everything subordinate to winning her; so you can perhaps understand a change in my ideas as regards science." In his *Autobiography* Roosevelt was to claim that his science classes at Harvard had dulled his interest, but certainly marriage to Alice Lee did not fit with three years of graduate study abroad followed by a life of research. At the same time he was attracted ever more to another field: "I shall probably either pursue a scientific course," he had recorded in his diary in August 1879, "or else study law, preparatory to going into public life." By the next spring it was decided: after their marriage in October 1880, the couple would move into 6 West 57th and Theodore would take up law studies at Columbia.

A career in public life had several attractions. His first course in political economy had proved so interesting that he had helped to found an undergraduate club that discussed current economic problems. Then Professor McLaughlin had advised him that political science offered more opportunities than natural history for worthwhile work. His prospective bride and her family would approve the choice, and his yearly income of $8,000 from his share of his father's estate would ease the financial liabilities of public service. At the very simplest level, Theodore was discovering that, like his father, he enjoyed people and their associations. In a more complex way, perhaps, he saw a life devoted to serving his fellow men as a way to honor his father's memory.

Theodore Roosevelt Senior had expressed his social

concern chiefly through his many philanthropies; he and others of his background had possessed too much taste and too little heart to engage actively in the politics of the Grant era. The one time he had become involved had been in November 1877, when President Rutherford B. Hayes, in a reform struggle with the New York Republican machine, had nominated him as collector of the port of New York. The bitter fight over that nomination in the United States Senate had profoundly disturbed the elder Theodore and possibly hastened his death several months later. At any rate the President had lost the battle; Senator Roscoe Conkling had defeated the reformers. And up in Cambridge, where he had watched it all in the newspapers, young Theodore had been "glad" on his father's account "but sorry for New York."

By 1880 it was not yet apparent that the son would find far more pleasure in political combat, but he had the father's set toward reform. It was the last of many endowments from a devoted parent. The young man who went around that winter to the meetings of the Republican Club of New York's Twenty-first District was striking out on his own. But in his buttonhole he could have worn a yellow saffronia rose.

II

"To Try to Amount to Something"

1880-1890

"I FEEL it incumbent on me to try to amount to something, either in politics or literature," Theodore Roosevelt wrote in July 1889, "because I have deliberately given up the hope of going into a money-making business."

Memories of his financial losses at cattle ranching in Dakota were painfully fresh, but his first two volumes on *The Winning of the West* were selling so well that the publisher thought there would soon have to be another edition. And though Theodore "mortally hated being so much away from home this summer," he really enjoyed his new post in Washington as a Civil Service commissioner.

"Of course however my political life is but an interlude," Roosevelt hastened to add, as he usually did in writing to his sisters. It was "quite impossible to continue long to do much," he concluded, "between two sets of such kittle-cattle as the spoilsmen and the mugwumps."

THE DIFFICULTIES ahead were mercifully hidden from the versatile young man who took up the law at Columbia in the fall of 1880. After a "perfect dream of delight" on their honeymoon at a country place at Oyster Bay, Theodore and Alice settled into his mother's West 57th Street house. Weekdays he usually walked the three miles downtown to Lafayette Place for lectures and study, followed often by a few steps around to the Astor Library for further research on his *Naval War of 1812*, a project begun in college after reading a British account which he considered grossly unfair to the American side. He was elected a trustee of the Orthopedic Dispensary, escorted Alice to countless parties and dances, and frequently on Sundays attended the Newsboys' dinner. He was taking up where his father had left off.

But one sign of the difference was the way in which young Theodore went regularly to meetings of the Republican Association of New York's Twenty-first District. Another sign came in the spring of 1881, when he fought unsuccessfully to get the Association to endorse a bill in the state legislature to reform the department of street cleaning. Theodore Roosevelt differed from others of his background and status in his willingness to mix actively with saloon keepers and ward heelers at the very base of the political structure. Within a week after returning from a summer trip to Europe, he was recording in his journal that in the upcoming primaries he was "going to try to kill our last year's legislator," the party hack from the Twenty-first who had voted against the street-cleaning bill at Albany.

That object just happened to appeal to Joseph Murray, a youthful lieutenant in Jake Hess's organization in the Twenty-first, who had his eye on Roosevelt as a worthy substitute for Hess's man. Murray gained Roosevelt the primary convention's endorsement and skillfully managed the ensuing campaign. Backed however reluctantly by the Hess machine, and strongly endorsed for his "high character . . . honesty and integrity" by such leading residents as Joseph H. Choate, Morris K. Jesup, and Elihu Root, in November 1881 Theodore Roosevelt was elected by a 1,500-vote majority.

"Too True! Too True! I have become a 'political hack,' " he wrote a college classmate. "But don't think I am going to go into politics after this year, for I am not."

Roosevelt's doubts about his political future were shared by the assemblymen and reporters who greeted the "dude" in Albany. This aristocrat with the gold fob excited a scornful mirth as he bounded into rooms silk hat in hand, exploded into such laughs that "his teeth seemed to be all over his face," and spoke out vigorously in his high-pitched cultivated accent. Roosevelt was "genial, emphatic, earnest," remarked the *Times* man, "but green as grass." The *Tribune* correspondent just shook his head: "What on earth will New York send us next?"

Roosevelt confided his critical comments on fellow legislators to his diary: "the average catholic Irishman of the first generation as represented in this Assembly, is a low, venal, corrupt and unintelligent brute," and in the committee on cities "most of the members are positively corrupt, and the others are really singularly incompetent." But his acid observations were scouting reports sizing up friend and foe while preparing the first sallies. The field was open to a stimulating contest. On the Republican side the ranks of the discredited Conkling machine were riddled with disaffection, while the Democratic majority had its troubles with the division between Tammany forces from New York City and the upstate regulars. Amid this party disarray an upright assemblyman could find on both sides independent-minded men with whom to work.

Roosevelt soon demonstrated that he had nothing against Irishmen or Catholics or even Democrats by cooperating with Mike Costello, from the Seventeenth New York, in research into every dubious proposal; their joint efforts were responsible for exposing a "steal" that would have reduced the taxes of certain elevated railways from 6 to 4 per cent. Able young Republicans like Isaac Hunt of Jefferson County recognized that this "most veritable representative of the New York dude" had the makings of a general for the campaign. On February 21, 1882, with Hunt and other antimachine men in support, Roosevelt scored his first tactical victory, defeating in caucus a Tammany "deal" with some of the G.O.P. leaders to take away the Speaker's power of appointment.

The bills Roosevelt introduced in 1882 were modest

reform measures; the only one to pass made the method of electing aldermen more understandable to the public. What really stamped him as the leader of the young reformers was his attempt to carry the impeachment of Judge Theodore Westbrook of the New York Supreme Court. Directed to this case initially by Ike Hunt, Roosevelt uncovered enough evidence of Westbrook's mishandling of receiverships to warrant introduction of a resolution empowering an investigation. This move aroused immediate opposition, for Westbrook had been involved with important business interests, including those of Jay Gould; by bold, clever tactics Roosevelt forced it through. Though a majority of the investigating committee eventually recommended against impeachment, a decision the Democrat-dominated chamber sustained despite heated protests, Roosevelt gained the support of leading New York papers (other than Gould's *World*) and of all the "young men of high character" in the assembly. It was an impressive finish to a dude's first session.

Roosevelt was "the most indiscreet guy I ever met," Ike Hunt recalled, "the most impulsive human being I ever knew." Country lawyers like Hunt did exercise a needed restraint upon their excitable colleague, yet the Westbrook affair had contained high drama. A family friend had tried to warn Roosevelt off the case, arguing that it endangered financial interests that were too important; the lobby had exerted all kinds of pressure; there had even been a blackmailing attempt to involve Roosevelt with a woman in distress on an Albany street.

Aggressive and combative, Theodore had been on his toes; "there wasn't anything cool about him," added Hunt, "and when they attacked him he would fire back with all the venom imaginable."

A few weeks after the session's close, Judge Westbrook died in a Troy hotel, but no one blamed Roosevelt; for the press and the politicians, the "dude" had simply "won his spurs." Such an appraisal recognized his increase in stature. With characteristic energy he had set out to inform himself on all aspects of state politics; he had been "a walking interrogation point," pinning men like Hunt with his probing questions, until Roosevelt knew more about political affairs in New York than did 90 per cent of the members. On week ends down in the City he had picked up new ideas; at Albany he had all but devoured the daily papers. "I think he grew faster than anybody I ever knew," recalled Hunt. "In those days, when he first started in there, I thought I knew more than he did, but before we got through he grew right away from me."

A testimonial dinner at Delmonico's made Roosevelt realize that his example was inspiring others ("It was like a splendid breeze blowing through the legislative halls," law student Charles Evans Hughes later recalled, "and making everyone feel brighter and better"), yet he was still testing his talents. On vacation from the summer's legal studies that September, he hesitated about buying a place there in upstate New York because it was so far from New York City. "Still, if I were perfectly certain that I would go on in politics and literature I should buy the farm without hesitation," he wrote, "but I consider the chances to be strongly favorable to my getting out of both — and if I intend to follow law or business I ought to stay in New York."

His uncertainty partly reflected the pessimistic outlook for the divided state G.O.P. in November. But Roosevelt survived the "Democratic Deluge" easily, carrying his assembly district by 2,200 votes. And since "nobody else seemed inclined to make the fight," Roosevelt presumed to enter the race for the Republican nomination for Speaker. He was sure to lose to a Democrat finally, yet his caucus election by a two-to-one margin was a signal honor. "My strength lay among the country Republicans, all of them native Americans, and for the most part farmers or storekeepers or small lawyers," he noted; "They are all shrewd, kindly, honest men, with whom I get on admirably."

The new minority leader went his own way in supporting civil service reform and higher liquor license fees and opposing state aid to sectarian institutions. He also showed his independence by reversing himself on the bill to require Jay Gould's Manhattan Railway Company to reduce its rush-hour fare from ten to the usual five cents. Gould's machinations had aroused press and public behind this measure, and Roosevelt voted with the majority to pass it 109 to 6, but when Governor Cleveland administered a well-reasoned veto, the minority leader at once changed his position, confessing "with shame that when I voted for this bill I did not act as I think I ought to have acted." "I weakly yielded," he told his amazed colleagues, "partly in a vindictive spirit toward the infernal thieves and conscienceless swindlers who have had the elevated road in charge and partly to the popular voice in New York."

However courageous, his words were hardly politic. He was not alone in his reversal, but most of those who switched were Democrats. Even his closest young allies refused to follow him. And from the papers on either side of the issue came criticisms; "the popular voice of New York," concluded the *Sun,* "will probably leave this weakling at home hereafter."

Smarting inwardly, Roosevelt struck back a week later in dramatic fashion. The committee on privileges and elections on which he served had earlier reported, by a vote of 7 to 2, that his Republican colleague from New York City, Henry L. Sprague, had been duly elected in November in a close contest. On March 8, however, to Roosevelt's astonishment, the assembly reversed the committee's verdict by a vote of 67 to 52. The next morning, rising to a question of privilege, the minority leader vented his rage upon "the Sodom and Gomorrah of the Democracy." The Democrats had shown "shameless partisanship." "I do not pretend to say that in latter times [my own party] has done all it ought to," he conceded, but "the difference between our party and yours is that your bad men throw out your good ones, while with us the good throw out the bad." To remain on the committee would be "simply a waste of my time," concluded Roosevelt, as he moved that his resignation be accepted. The assembly rejected his motion and moved on to other business, but the reaction of the opposition press betrayed a well-developed opinion at Albany that the minority "leader" was too impressed with his own importance and much too self-righteous. Twenty years later, Theodore confessed that in 1883 "I came an awful cropper, and had to pick myself up after learning by bitter experience that I was not all-important and that I had to take account of many different elements in life."

Roosevelt did not lower his moral standard: his personal judgments remained as vigorous as ever. However, he learned again and again in the following decade that "political action, to be effective, must be the joint action of many men," and that the reformer "must sacrifice somewhat of his own opinions to those of his associates if he ever hopes to see his desires take practical shape." The gospel of morality had to be coordinated with the gospel of efficiency. To be efficient, a party leader could not be brash and self-opinionated.

At Albany Roosevelt also gained invaluable experience with problems affecting capital and labor. At Harvard he had absorbed a *laissez-faire* philosophy that conformed with his father's views on self-help; in fact, these attitudes had led young Theodore too far toward advocacy of free trade for his subsequent comfort within his party. But in the Westbrook case and in a bill prohibiting cigar manufacture in tenements, Roosevelt found his theories challenged by facts. Too much the scientist to ignore hard evidence, he had to adjust his perspective.

He did not condemn all businessmen or all men of great wealth, but simply "the wealthy criminal class." A man like Jay Gould, who obtained improper favors through Judge Westbrook, deserved the censure of the community. A firm like Gould's Manhattan Railway Company, sneaking a tax reduction through the legislature, deserved exposure by vigilant lawmakers. To Roosevelt it was clear that business was involved with government; that it was wrong to exploit that relationship in any corrupt way, either by bribing legislators or by extorting blackmail from corporations; and that measures should, if possible, not discriminate among companies in the same field. What was not so obvious to him was what should be done about conflicts of interests, as between utilities and the public, or between employers and laboringmen.

Labor was difficult for him to understand. More and more workingmen through concerted action were attacking the abuses of the new industrial system; in strike-bound plants and legislative halls they were seeking remedies for workdays of twelve and thirteen hours, for wages that would not feed their children, for working conditions that incapacitated some and brutalized others. Paeans to self-help grated on their ears, yet their strikes roused a chorus of bourgeois protest. Members from their districts usually supported them in legislatures, but they were already underrepresented, and union lobbyists only antagonized men like Roosevelt through crude appeals. "Professional agitators," he would write in 1885, were "always promising to procure by legislation the advantages which can only come to workingmen . . . by their individual or united energy, intelligence, and forethought."

Roosevelt's opposition to Tammany explained his opposition in 1882 to higher salaries for New York City's firemen and policemen and to a minimum wage for laborers employed by cities. But he was generally unresponsive to labor's demands. In 1883, in criticizing the proposal of the Hatters' Union to do away with competing manufacture in state prisons, he showed more solicitude for the taxpayer than for free labor. The next year, in speaking against a bill to limit the workday of street-car conductors to twelve hours, he argued that it would impair their self-reliance by tying them to the apron strings of the state. The twelve-hour bill passed both houses, only to be vetoed by the conservative Grover Cleveland as "class legislation."

The measure to prohibit the manufacture of cigars in tenements forced Roosevelt for the first time to adjust his theories to the facts. His initial reaction to this bill was hostile, in keeping with the business view that it would "prevent a man doing as he wished and as he had a right to do with what was his own." At the invitation of Samuel Gompers of the Cigarmakers' International, however, he toured the miserable slum apartments where immigrant Bohemian families labored fifteen and sixteen hours a day turning out a third of New York's annual production of 700 million cigars. Upset by such conditions, Roosevelt led the two other members of his tenements subcommittee on a similar tour and came away convinced that "whatever the theories might be, as a matter of practical common sense I could not conscientiously vote for the continuance of the conditions which I saw."

Roosevelt's support assisted the bill through the assembly in 1882, and again in 1883, when it finally went to the governor. Cleveland, dubious about signing it, called a hearing at which Roosevelt appeared as spokesman for the workers. "He said that his district was not influenced by any trade unions, and that he was opposed to most of their measures, but this bill was an exception to the rule." The facts Roosevelt presented swayed Cleveland's judgment, but not that of the judiciary. Ruling against the law first on a technicality that required repassage in the 1884 session, the Court of Appeals finally declared it unconstitutional; the judges could not see "how the cigarmaker is to be improved in his health or his morals by forcing him from his home and its hallowed associations and beneficent influences to ply his trade elsewhere."

This *Jacobs* decision, Roosevelt later testified, "first waked me to a dim and partial understanding of the fact that the courts were not necessarily the best judges of what should be done to better social and industrial conditions." It was an understanding similar to that he derived from his legal studies: "some of the teaching of the lawbooks and of the classroom seemed to me to be against justice." Roosevelt would not go on in the law.

This flexibility was a portent of the future; for the present, Roosevelt only knew that the strain of the 1883 session had worn him down. Early that summer, asthma and general indisposition drove him to the healing waters of Richfield Springs, but he was "bored out of my life" among "underbred and overdressed girls, fat old female scandal mongers, and a select collection of assorted

cripples and consumptives." A better remedy, one which
had worked three years before in 1880, was to go west on
a hunting trip. Theodore headed after big game in Dakota. On September 20, 1883, after a long pursuit that
left Roosevelt "plumb tired out," he shot his first buffalo.
It seemed a good sign: the day before, he had written a
check for $14,000 as his initial investment in a ranch herd
in the Bad Lands.

This venture was not impulsive. The area was just beginning to develop, prospects for successful ranching
seemed bright, and his new partners, with whom he had
talked for days, were reliable and experienced. Beyond
that, Roosevelt had clearly begun his romance with the
West. The lonely grandeur of the scenery, the rugged
life of the frontier, the easy democratic ways of the set-
tlers — all captured him. The West filled a need in his
nature; with a financial stake there, he was doubly certain to return. Quite incidentally, he thereby became one
of those rare Eastern politicians with an appeal that could
be called national.

Reinvigorated by adventure, Roosevelt plunged back
into New York politics. The state G.O.P. did well
enough that November to carry both houses, so he
launched a spirited campaign for the party nomination
for Speaker, but this time his machine opponents were
equally active. Roosevelt accepted the narrow defeat
philosophically: he was the new chairman of the committee on cities, he was preparing a reform bill centralizing
greater power in the mayor's office, and Alice was expect-
ing their first child in February. "I love you and long for

you all the time, and oh *so* tenderly; doubly tenderly now, my sweetest little wife," he wrote from Albany on February 6, 1884. "I just long for Friday evening when I shall be with you again."

A daughter, Alice Lee, was born on February 12; on February 14, in the same house at 6 West 57th, Roosevelt's mother died of typhoid fever and his wife succumbed to Bright's disease. "There *is* a curse on this house," Theodore muttered. And then his mind closed upon his beloved bride. He was never to speak of her to their child, nor would he mention her in his autobiography. His was the grief of silence.

The same discipline drove him back to work; "indeed," he wrote, "I think I should go mad if I were not employed." That spring was perhaps the busiest Roosevelt ever spent in politics. He pushed to a conclusion a broad investigation of the government of New York City. He also saw through to enactment six out of nine reform bills to eliminate waste and corruption from municipal administration. At one point, exasperated at delays, he became so peremptory that some called him arrogant. "I am not arrogant," Roosevelt told a reporter, "I am simply in dead earnest." The new gospel of efficiency allied to morality achieved results.

That spring was the busier because Roosevelt, as the acknowledged leader of the reform forces in the state party, was involved in preparations for the national convention in June. Because of their unsavoury records, neither Chester A. Arthur nor James G. Blaine was an acceptable presidential candidate for Roosevelt, who early indicated his preference for Senator George F. Edmunds of Vermont, a colorless but eminently respectable figure who had strong backing in New England. Elected a delegate to the state convention at Utica in April, Roosevelt directed the smaller Edmunds forces to a "mainly accidental success": the larger Arthur group, out of fear of Blaine, came over to support Roosevelt and three other Edmunds men as delegates-at-large to Chicago. "There, damn you," Roosevelt shouted at the leader of the Blaine faction, who had engineered the Speakership defeat in January, "we beat you for last winter."

Roosevelt's triumph was brief, but he threw himself conspicuously into the anti-Blaine movement. He tried to drum up strength in the Middle West through Benjamin Harrison's manager in Indiana. With Henry Cabot Lodge of Massachusetts, he conferred with E. L. Godkin and other independents in New York and Washington. At Chicago he visited one delegation after another, explored possible bargains with Ohio's Sherman backers, stayed "up all night in arranging our forces so as to get the different factions to come in to line together to defeat the common foe." It was all in vain, for "the second choice of all of the Logan and Sherman and of nearly half the Arthur men," as Roosevelt found out, "was Blaine, which made it absolutely impossible to form a combination against him."

In the aftermath of defeat Roosevelt was so bitter that he may have said that any proper Democratic nomination would have the independent Republicans' support, but within two days, on his way west, he was denying he

had, and within ten days he was writing Lodge "I agree
with you heartily in thinking that, unless very good cause
— more than we now know — can be shown, we can take
part in no bolt." A month later Cleveland was the Democratic nominee, and some of the independent leaders with
whom Roosevelt had worked so closely had deserted the
G.O.P., but Roosevelt refused to join George William
Curtis, Carl Schurz, and other "mugwumps." He con-
tented himself at first with the thought that he would not
"take any part whatever in the campaign — indeed, I
may be in Dakota on election day," but as the fall contest
approached he chafed at this compromise; increasingly
critical of Cleveland's record as governor, he longed to be
"battling along with" Cabot Lodge, who was running
for Congress. At last he could remain aloof no longer; he
returned east to do what he could to get "all independent Republicans to support the Republican ticket."

The stand Roosevelt took in speeches that fall in New
York and Boston failed to elect Blaine or Lodge, but it
confirmed his split with many independents he once led.
He had solved his cruel dilemma as a politician must, if
he expects to remain in politics; and if he went further
than he needed, it was mostly because he resented so
keenly the mugwump claim to a superior moral position.
In future major elections he would show a similar tend-
ency to lean too far toward the regulars, in resentment
at the independents, but his basic position was akin to
that he had evolved in the assembly. It was not enough to
be moral; to be efficient the true reformer had to work
within a party, with all kinds of men, including some
(Blaine!) of far lower ideals than his own.

The stance between the spoilsmen and the mugwumps would never be easy, but in Henry Cabot Lodge the campaign of 1884 provided a firm friend who would share the difficulties. A fellow Porcellian and son of an importer, a literary man and a skilled horseman, the indefatigable Lodge had a background and interests so similar to Roosevelt's that the two might have become boon companions in any event; their political ordeal cemented the relation. Eight years the senior, and more cautiously calculating in temperament, Lodge supplied a valuable check to Roosevelt's instincts; in time he would also be in a position to advance Roosevelt's career. In November 1884 it was Roosevelt who consoled ("come back in time you must and will") and counselled ("don't let the Independents see you express any chagrin") the "Dear old fellow."

Afflicted by personal tragedy and party misfortune, Roosevelt had not stood for reelection; he retired from active politics, and his ranching interests afforded an ideal escape. There on the western plain the harsh memories would fade in his mind, his body would harden in new strength. He would have time to ride and hunt, and to work with Bill Sewall and his nephew, who had come on from Maine, in cutting logs for the new ranch house at the Elkhorn. He would have time, too, for writing; he was beginning to assemble photographs and stories for his *Hunting Trips of a Ranchman*, and in January 1885 he'd have a long article in *Century* on "Phases of State Legislation." Back in New York for Christmas with his family, he would be off again in March 1885 for Dakota to ride like any cowboy in the spring roundup. In July, more rugged-looking than ever, he would return to check corrections on his book and move his possessions at last into the twelve-bedroom house he and Alice had planned at Oyster Bay; its walls decorated with his many trophies, "Leeholm," renamed "Sagamore," would give him a comfortable base in the east. In late August he would find the ranch house that was his western base more homelike also, in the capable hands of Mrs. Sewall and Dow's new wife. By the time the Republican state convention assembled at Saratoga in September 1885, Roosevelt would be on hand to do what he could for the reform forces, but he would show no inclination to run himself. He would still be in a mood to say "I do not expect to return to politics for many years, if at all."

The squire of Sagamore found an obvious pleasure in riding with neighboring gentlemen in the Meadowbrook Hunt that fall of 1885; not so obvious was his enchantment with a friend from childhood, Edith Carow, to whom he became secretly engaged in November. Before college his letters had often referred to his love for Edith, who was particularly close to his sister Corinne, and after his marriage he had continued to see her occasionally; at Alice's death, the relationship abruptly terminated. Theodore's determination to be constant to Alice's memory reinforced his regard for propriety; he deliberately tried to avoid Edith. But one day in October a chance encounter at his older sister's weakened his resolve. Soon they were in love.

Thinking it still too soon to wed, they finally agreed that Edith should proceed with previous plans to go abroad in the spring with her mother, while Theodore returned to Dakota in March to tend to his business affairs. Meanwhile he had his literary work: he was beginning to collect materials from Lyman C. Draper and others for his study of *The Winning of the West*, and in February 1886 he accepted an offer to do *Thomas Hart Benton* for the American Statesman series. To Cabot Lodge, who was doing *George Washington* and had suggested Roosevelt to the editor, Theodore admitted "I will be delighted when I get settled down to work of some sort again."

Once back in Dakota in March 1886, Roosevelt professed to be enjoying himself and to have little interest in his political career. Yet when the mayor of New York City sounded him out about taking the presidency of the board of health, Roosevelt was inclined to accept, though Lodge thought the job beneath his dignity. When a border incident strained relations with Mexico, Roosevelt wrote the Secretary of War "offering to try to raise some companies of horse riflemen." "I haven't the least idea there will be any trouble," he wrote Lodge, "but as my chance of doing anything in the future worth doing seems to grow continually smaller I intend to grasp at every opportunity that turns up."

Opportunity of a sort turned up in the fall of 1886, as the New York Republicans, casting about for a candidate to run for mayor, finally approached Roosevelt. It was an unpromising offer, for the real opponent of the Democrats' able and wealthy Abram S. Hewitt would be the single-taxer Henry George, author of *Progress and*

Poverty, who headed the United Labor ticket. Roosevelt realized that it was "a perfectly hopeless contest," but he accepted for the good of the party, and he made an excellent showing, polling 60,435 votes against 68,110 for George and 90,552 for Hewitt. Too many Republicans, rejecting Roosevelt's effort to minimize the "class" threat from George, had crossed party lines to vote for Hewitt. Too many independents, rejecting Roosevelt's understandable protests, had regarded the G.O.P. slate as "a mere mixture of straw, put up by the Republican machine ring in the interest of Tammany Hall." But he had made a "rattling canvass," and at least had "a better party standing than ever before."

The harsh winter that descended over the western plains in November also thrust Roosevelt back into politics. Low beef prices had already made many ranchers financially vulnerable; Roosevelt's expenses so far exceeded his income that in January, on their honeymoon trip in Italy after a London wedding, he and Edith were thinking "very seriously of selling Sagamore Hill and going to the ranch for a year or two." Then deep snows and bitter cold dashed the hopes for holding on in the west. The damage to his herd was "even worse than I feared; I wish I was sure I would lose no more than half the money ($80,000) I invested out here," he wrote in April 1887 from Dakota. "I am planning how to get out of it."

Though eventually his losses proved less than expected, and though he had inherited an additional $62,-500 at his mother's death, Roosevelt's style of living produced a financial pinch that whetted his desire to "amount to something." His books enhanced his income and reputation, yet even as he drove himself ("Writing is horribly hard work to me") to produce, it was apparent that, as with Lodge, Roosevelt's main interest was politics and public policy. His *Benton* was chiefly notable for his vigorous endorsement of westward expansion; at the same time he condemned the spoils system, endorsed hard money, championed the Union, and attacked the abolitionists for their extremism ("It was not written to please those political and literary hermaphrodites the mugwumps"). His *Gouverneur Morris,* completed in 1887 for the same series, lauded the Federalists for their sound economic policies but sharply criticized their opposition to the westward movement and the War of 1812. His *Winning of the West*, while incomparably better history, revealed in its contempt for the Jeffersonians the same active partisanship that marked Roosevelt's campaigning.

Roosevelt best showed his bent in a *Century* article in November 1886 on "Machine Politics in New York City," in which he contrasted "the clockwork regularity and efficiency" of the political machines with "THE NEGLECT OF PUBLIC DUTIES BY RESPECTABLE MEN IN EASY CIRCUMSTANCES." He exemplified the "manlier virtues" himself by continuing his work within the Twenty-first District Association. And once back in the East, he began to take an active part in the Federal and Union League Clubs.

With Lodge elected to Congress in 1886, and with the approach of the 1888 campaign, Roosevelt manifested a

greater interest in national issues. The ultraprotection-
ists, he feared, would turn the G.O.P. into "a mere party
of reaction" if they disposed of the embarrassing treasury
surplus by abolishing the whiskey tax and approving too-
generous pensions. A part of the surplus, he contended
in a minority report at the Union League, should go to
"building a navy and providing adequate coast defence."
And though Democratic schemes for broad tariff reduc-
tions were "ludicrous," the Republicans would be just as
wrong to insist that "maintenance of the present tariff
unchanged with all its anomalies was a point to which
every other interest and issue should be subordinated."

When Benjamin Harrison was nominated, Roosevelt
dutifully offered his services to the national committee.
When the call came for a twelve-day speaking tour
through Michigan and Minnesota, he cheerfully forsook
polo and his book to respond. "I can't help thinking that
this time we have our foes on the hip," he remarked
upon his return. On election day Cleveland won a popular majority, but Harrison captured the electoral vote,
233 to 168.

Republican victory opened opportunities for appointment in the new government, but Roosevelt suppressed
his hopes in anxiety about a wholesale removal of federal
officeholders. He thought his party justified in removing
"Mr. Cleveland's more vicious and incompetent appointees," but he opposed a sweep of the fourth-class postmasters and came out boldly for an extension of the
classified service. Hopeful that more reformers would
take a practical line, in February 1889 at Baltimore he

presented his case to a national conference of civil service reform leaders. Anxious that the spoilsmen would not embarrass him with the mugwumps, he protested strongly at Harrison's intended replacement of the able postmaster of New York City with an "ordinary ward politician," a henchman of Thomas C. Platt, the boss of the state machine. "I do hope the President will appoint good civil service commissioners," Roosevelt confided to Lodge in April; "I am very much discontented with him so far."

Lodge, meantime, had been urging Roosevelt's appointment as Assistant Secretary of State, but the new Secretary, James G. Blaine, thought "so brilliant and aggressive a man" unsuited to a post requiring "the most thoughtful concentration and the most stubborn inaction." Roosevelt's reaction to Lodge's "absolutely unexpected" overtures indicated that he had his own reservations about taking a post under Blaine, but that he "would have particularly liked to have been in Washington, in an official position, while you [Lodge] were in Congress." In April 1889 Harrison finally agreed to name the young New Yorker one of the three United States Civil Service commissioners.

"I hated to take the place," Roosevelt wrote, "but I hardly thought I ought to refuse." His reluctance reflected the difficulties he foresaw: the commissioners could only make enemies among politicians, yet any laxity would arouse the vigilant reformers. For Roosevelt, however, this was a familiar and really inescapable dilemma. In fact, his stern code peculiarly suited him to enforce a law whose purpose he endorsed so heartily. "For the last few years politics with me has been largely a balancing of evils," he observed most revealingly in July 1889, "and I am delighted to go in on a side where I have no doubt whatever, and feel absolutely certain that my efforts are wholly for the good."

Roosevelt had already experienced his crucial baptism in fire. The assembly had tested him, and he had emerged a seasoned leader. The Blaine nomination had tried him so sorely that he had retreated from the field, but he had come back with a more effective stance. Never one to shirk a good fight, Roosevelt had found political warfare challenging. He was ready for Washington.

III

"Fit for That Great Trust"

1890-1900

THE NATION would be shocked in September 1901 at the sudden turn of fate that brought to the Presidency the youngest man to occupy that seat of power until then. Conservatives would express gratitude that this forty-two-year-old leader proposed to continue the slain President's policies, and the editor of the Hartford *Times* would voice a confidence supported by the record.

"If a man were to be put into training for the duties of the presidential office in his boyhood," the *Times* would declare, "we do not see how any course could be mapped out for him which would be more likely to make him fit for that great trust than that through which the new President has so rapidly and so creditably passed."

It could seem in 1901 that there almost had been a plan to Roosevelt's progress through his various posts as assemblyman, Civil Service commissioner, police commissioner of New York City, Assistant Secretary of the Navy, colonel in the Rough Riders, governor of New York, and Vice-President. Certainly he had gained experience at all levels of government. He had developed skill as a lawmaker and particularly as an administrator. He had dealt with foreign as well as domestic issues, and had debated national policies on stumps east and west. Only insiders like Lodge knew the roads not taken, the fortuitous moves along that path; yet Lodge also knew how he and others had schemed to advance Theodore's interests.

ONE CRITICAL POINT had come in the fall of 1894, when Roosevelt had been five years in Washington. He had about completed what he wanted to do as Civil Service commissioner, when there came an unexpected offer to put him up for mayor of New York on a reform-fusion ticket. With Tammany in disrepute, it seemed a promising opportunity. But his wife Edith feared the financial damage of a losing race, so Theodore declined without consulting his older sister or Cabot. "I made a mistake in not trying my luck in the mayoralty race," he soon confessed, "but it is hard to decide when one has the interests of a wife and children to consider first."

The next year the new mayor, at the urging principally of journalist-politician Lemuel E. Quigg, appointed Roosevelt police commissioner. Roosevelt performed capably, although his reform measures antagonized the Platt machine to such an extent that the Republican majority in the state government threatened to legislate him out of office. Senator Lodge came to the rescue and persuaded President William McKinley and Secretary of the Navy John D. Long to name Roosevelt Assistant Secretary.

Theodore's most fateful decision of the decade came a year later, with the conflict for which he had tried to prepare the fleet. He had advocated war with Spain so wholeheartedly that he thought it would be dishonorable to stay behind. Several of his six children had been ill, and Edith was still recovering from an operation, but Theodore felt the call of duty too strongly to resist; if he didn't return, he told one friend, at least his estate would see the youngsters through their education.

The colonel of the Rough Riders did return in August 1898, a popular hero of the Cuban battles, to find the G.O.P. in New York fortuitously in need of his services as a gubernatorial candidate. A scandal over improvements to the Erie Canal had so discredited the incumbent that Boss Platt was willing to take on this reformer, once assured that war on the machine would not result. Roosevelt campaigned hard and won, and once in office he faithfully consulted organization leaders on policies and appointments, yet inevitably there were clashes, particularly over a franchise-tax bill he helped to push through, and over his refusal to reappoint a corrupt machine lieutenant as superintendent of insurance. Though his administration redeemed the party's reputation in the state, and though Roosevelt indicated that he wanted to stand for reelection in 1900, Platt wanted a man more acceptable to the regulars and to the conservative business community.

The last step in this remarkable "progress" toward the

Presidency came at the Republican national convention at Philadelphia in June 1900. Against Lodge's advice, Roosevelt battled right into the convention hall to keep from being named McKinley's running mate, protesting the while privately that he would have too little to do as Vice-President, that McKinley's mantle would not clearly fall on him there in 1904, that the governorship would be a far better place to remain in the presidential contention. His efforts failed, his resistance collapsed before a wave of boss-supported eastern and spontaneous western sentiment that McKinley's manager Mark Hanna himself could not contain. "In caucus I upset Senator Platt and stood the New York machine on its head, forcing them to vote for somebody else," Roosevelt informed one friend disturbed by talk of Platt's coup, "but outside of New York the demand for me was due to genuine regard and belief in my strength."

If Platt thought he had disposed of Roosevelt by "kicking him upstairs," the fatal shooting of September 1901 was a shattering blow, which illumined the pattern in Roosevelt's advancement. New York had always been his political base, but the organization leaders there had never made his way easy; they had assisted him to office only when he could be of use, had fought with him when he threatened their interests, had forced him onto the national administration whenever they conveniently could. Unable to control the attitude of the people toward Roosevelt, they had nevertheless sought to manipulate him to their purposes. In so doing, they had contributed to the zig-zag effect in this progress. They had also contributed, paradoxically and unwittingly, to his mounting strength.

The difficulties of his position in New York shaped Roosevelt's attitude toward his own career. Though intensely ambitious for place and desirous of power, he was customarily pessimistic about attaining either. More than that, he conceived a positive distaste for talking about his future, not only because the hazards were great, but because concern about the possible effects of some action might produce too much expediency. His assembly days had taught him that some adjustment to others' standards was necessary; but, as he put it in 1885, "No man can do good service in the Legislature as long as he is worrying over the effect of his actions upon his own future." He often remarked, "how many men have I seen ruined by getting the presidential bee in their bonnets."

Fear of his own ambition caused Roosevelt to protest too much; it did not keep him from taking elementary precautions. When he arrived in Washington in 1889, for example, he used his last two calling cards on the Blaines and on Matthew S. Quay, chairman of the Republican National Committee and a dominant figure in Pennsylvania; within a year or so there were few politicians on the national scene Roosevelt had not at least met. When the intra-party struggle in New York was particularly bitter, moreover, as in the municipal election of 1897, he was relieved that his position in the McKinley administration kept him from taking an active part.

Yet considerations of personal expediency affected him comparatively little. In enforcing the law he did not discriminate between parties. In fighting for a policy in which he believed, he usually did not stop to reckon the cost to himself. In elections he tempered morality more readily to the demands of the moment; biennially he succumbed to the view that if the Democracy prevailed, disaster would strike. But within the G.O.P. he never ceased to contend for principle against place, for devotion to good government against mere party success.

Such an approach was eminently suited to his own situation. His neglect of expediency was not just a sign of pessimism about getting along with the machine. Nor was it just a reflection of financial and social security. It showed some awareness of the fact that his real strength rested with the people, the bulk of whom appreciated frankness and admired courageous stands, however much some of them might at times disagree. Without popular support the politicians would have made short shrift of him.

The popular image of Roosevelt as a brave champion of reform grew stronger through the 1890's. Each post he held presented a challenging opportunity to work for more efficient government; each had its frustrations. In each Roosevelt developed his particular style of investigating and publicizing issues; in each he learned lessons in greater restraint. And always he added significantly to his resources, in sheer knowledge and informed friends.

The great challenge to the Civil Service commission

in 1889 was to enforce an inadequate law with inadequate means in the face of a horde of Republican patronage seekers. The outgoing administration had made the
task more difficult by extending the bounds of the classified service, the perimeter of which reached into many
post offices and customs houses across the land. Gaps
within the defenses were wide, for promotions were not
covered, and removals were not as clearly under the regulations as appointments. Furthermore, the clerical force
was too small and incompetent to handle the hundreds
of thousands of letters and examinations that flooded the
Washington office each year.

Roosevelt at once solicited the aid of prominent civil
service reformers in reporting and repairing any
breaches in the system. In company with the able Democratic member of the commission, he also "administered
a galvanic shock" to the outposts by a personal tour of
Indianapolis, Chicago, Milwaukee, and Grand Rapids.
On-the-spot investigations, launched often by surprise,
became a regular feature of Roosevelt's methods. He got
in equally good blows in Washington, standing up to
congressmen and department heads who were tolerating
or conniving at violations, agitating constantly for larger
appropriations and more rigorous regulations, defending
always the practical merit of the civil service idea.

Praise from mugwumps and plaints from spoilsmen
soon warned that such efforts might go too far for his
own good, but Roosevelt became increasingly exasperated with timid, half-hearted support from the Harrison administration. "I suppose a half-and-half, bone-

less policy, may be safe; I hope so, most sincerely," he
wrote, "but it is neither ennobling nor inspiring."
Roosevelt soon believed that Harrison's "one anxiety is
not to have anything [to do] with us or the Civil Service
Law." Even when the President adopted more stringent
rules regarding examinations, and at least introduced the
competitive principle into promotions, Roosevelt remained dissatisfied because neither step went as far as the
commission had recommended. "He has never given us
one ounce of real backing," Roosevelt remarked more re-
sentfully than accurately in July 1891. "It is horribly
disheartening to work under such a Chief."

The young commissioner's impatience annoyed a be-
leaguered Harrison, who once complained that Roosevelt "wanted to put an end to all the evil in the world
between sunrise and sunset." But Harrison soon had
greater cause for concern at Roosevelt's impending clash
with Postmaster General John Wanamaker over the Baltimore post office. An avowed partisan who had replaced
some 30,000 postmasters, Wanamaker had removed
Baltimore's Democratic postmaster in 1889 with the commission's blessing, but two years later Roosevelt, in investigating a hotly contested Republican primary in
that city, had found enough evidence of arbitrary removals and improper political assessments to recommend that twenty-five federal appointees be dismissed.
Harrison had laid this report aside while Wanamaker
sent his own inspectors down; by October 1891, amid
"rumors of my own removal," Roosevelt was bristling
at press stories that the Postmaster General "intends to
'Prove the falsity' of my report."

As month after month passed without publication of either report, Roosevelt's forebearance wore so thin that he began to defend himself in press interviews and reform meetings; at length he demanded and got an inquiry by the House Civil Service committee. A majority of the Democratic-controlled committee eventually found in his favor, but not before days of investigation, including sharp exchanges between Roosevelt and Wanamaker, had laid open the whole affair. "Such a muss" may have contributed something to the Republican defeat in November, but however impolitic, the publicity served the cause of civil service reform. And Roosevelt became so identified with that cause that Cleveland kept him on until May 1895. By then the commission's work was "proceeding so well" and its position was "established on so firm a basis," that Roosevelt felt "no doubt as to the future of the cause."

In 1895 the police commission offered as great a challenge to his particular skills. The same corruption that Roosevelt had uncovered in the 1884 probe still disgraced the ranks, whose chief, the famous detective Thomas F. Byrnes, admitted to personal gains of $350,-000, obtained, he said, through stock market tips from Jay Gould. The same kind of four-man bipartisan board that Roosevelt in 1884 had wanted to replace with a single commissioner still throttled efficiency. Tammany and the local Republicans still coveted and shared the police power, the state legislature still interfered for partisan ends, although the Lexow investigation had roused the city to put in an anti-Tammany ticket pledged to reform.

Chosen president at the first meeting of the newly constituted board, Roosevelt set to work as if he expected to
reorganize the force in two months. Checking tirelessly
over records almost every day until six, he soon forced
out the admittedly skilled Byrnes because "I thoroughly
distrust him, and cannot do any thorough work while he
remains." Then a police inspector accused of graft and
incompetence resigned, and a month after taking office
Roosevelt made the first of several surprise forays by
night to inspect performance. "A good many were not
doing their duty," he wrote, "and I had a line of huge
frightenned [sic] guardians of the peace down for repri-
mand or fine, as a sequel to my all-night walk."

His whirlwind pace and dramatic deeds made head-
lines. Roosevelt was "rather amused at the way I have become for the moment rather a prominent personage."
But he ran into an "ugly snag" in the state law prohibiting the sale of alcoholic beverages on Sunday. No pro-
hibitionist himself, he acknowledged privately that this
law was "altogether too strict," but until the legislature
modified it he had "no honorable alternative save to enforce it, and I *am* enforcing it, to the furious rage of the
saloon keepers, and of many good people too; for which
I am sorry." That summer would have thirsty Sundays
for many workingmen, and that fall the German-Americans would wreak particular vengeance on the G.O.P.,
but Roosevelt resolutely held his ground, not just because he thought it an "impregnable" position morally
and logically, but because any weakening would compromise his general effort to render New York's Finest
incorruptible.

Encouraged by signs of support the nation over, Roosevelt even contended that his stand was politically expedient, but the city Republicans equivocated on the issue, the Good Government forces broke off support of fusion, and Tammany, exploiting any act that seemed to discriminate against the poorer people, made large gains in November. By 1896 Roosevelt found himself in difficulty with many Republican leaders city and state.

Above all, troubles appeared in that clumsy administrative device, the bipartisan commission, where one man often could forestall effective action. In the summer of 1895, annoyed perhaps at Roosevelt's prominence and certainly encouraged by the machine leaders, the other Republican member, Frederick D. Grant, began to object to Sunday Law enforcement. Worse yet, the anti-Tammany Democrat Andrew D. Parker began to play a devious game in blocking major promotions (which required unanimity) and collaborating with the Platt organization (to stop a reform bill to permit promotions by majority vote). By June 1896 Parker's neglect of duty brought him to trial, but the mayor did not remove him until March 1897. In that interval the board only inched ahead through "interminable wrangling"; as Roosevelt finally admitted, "Grant and Parker between them have brought the affairs of the Police Department into an utter snarl."

"With proper power," he had written Lodge a year before, "I could make this Department of the first rank from top to bottom." But though he had chafed at the system's restrictions, the board under his leadership had cleaned up the force, had set up an examining board and a probationary period, and had eliminated religious and political considerations from appointments and promotions. Through the publicity which these efforts had received, citizens in many cities troubled with the same problems had taken heart; the image of Roosevelt the reformer had taken a firmer hold on the popular imagination. The middle-class professional and business men who would lead the progressive movement had been impressed with the performance.

The Navy Department offered an equally good opportunity for practical if less spectacular work. More than that, it afforded Roosevelt an unusual chance to implement foreign policy views long in the making. For he saw the navy as the primary means by which America had to assert and defend its place as an emerging world power. He was therefore eager to do all he could to fit this vital arm for its decisive role. The service had to be ready; when war came, it would be too late to prepare.

Roosevelt's intense devotion to this new task was rooted in militant nationalism. The Franco-Prussian War had awakened Europe from mid-century dreams of a harmonious free-trading concert of free nations under Great Britain's benign hegemony. A unified, powerful, autocratic Germany thereafter challenged England's eminence and threatened the balance of power. Nationalism grew harsh and militant as it was infused with fears of exclusion from valuable markets, and with the persuasive theory that survival in the struggle of nations, as of men, went to the fittest. Christian apologists joined racists in justifying the extension of civilized rule over the world's backward peoples.

Combative by instinct and early training, and recep-
tive to the new ideas by reason of the Civil War influence
and scientific studies, Roosevelt readily fell in step with
nationalistic forces in his own party and country. He retained his free-trade bias, but he parted company with
influential reformers of an older generation, like E. L.
Godkin of the *Nation*, who continued to oppose flag-
waving nationalism and imperialism and war. After
1884, when many of these enlightened leaders turned
mugwump, Roosevelt found added reason to oppose
them. The Democracy he associated with disunion; it
would be logical, he reasoned, for men of a weak, pacific
disposition to go over to that side.

The party of Lincoln, on the other hand, had saved
the nation, and true republicans (Roosevelt often used
the small "r") should be proud of this great country
and its institutions. That pride made him "intensely
anti-anglomaniac," resentful of British superiority, real
or fancied, and sharply critical of the "colonialism" of
too many American writers ("Thank Heaven Henry
James is now an avowedly British novelist"). It shaped
his historical interests and judgments, his exaltation of
the West and the robust manly Westerner, his belief that
Americans were more moral than Europeans, his con-
tentions that the immigrant should leave off Old World
ways and that the Catholic should try to Americanize
his church. Extraordinarily conscious of any threat to
the country's unity, Roosevelt hoped that the melting
pot of American life would somehow continue to weld
diverse origins into a vigorous, wholesome composite.
He hoped that literary men would assist that process by

celebrating the native scene and character, and particularly that they would not turn "decadent" and critical and pessimistic as William Dean Howells and Hamlin Garland had.

Ardent nationalism passed easily into bristling militancy in a man who admired strength and acted on what he believed. In Captain A. T. Mahan's *The Influence of Sea Power upon History, 1660-1783* (1890) Roosevelt found an expansionist rationale to frame his martial patriotism. Mahan argued from England's rise to power that to compete successfully in the vital struggle for world markets a nation needed a large merchant marine protected by a navy with battle-fleet supremacy. By 1898 Mahan would contend more explicitly that such supremacy for America would require an isthmian canal defended by Caribbean and Pacific bases. Roosevelt and Lodge admired his ideas and tried to get the scholarly captain reassigned in 1893 to the Naval War College. "It is a great misfortune," Roosevelt was writing in May 1894, "that we have not annexed Hawai [*sic*]; gone on with our navy, and started an interoceanic canal at Nicaragua."

Roosevelt's jingoistic nationalism swelled with the Cleveland administration's vigorous defense of the Monroe Doctrine against Britain the next year in the Venezuela boundary dispute. Already a strong believer "in ultimately driving every European power off this continent," Roosevelt almost hoped England would be provoked into war. "Let the fight come if it must; I don't care whether our sea coast cities are bombarded or not," he declared; "we would take Canada." "The antics of the bankers, brokers and anglomaniacs generally," the protests of "our peace at any price men" at Harvard and elsewhere so irritated him that he took up his pen in Cleveland's defense in *The Harvard Crimson*. "A temperate but resolute insistence upon our rights is the surest way to secure peace," Roosevelt reasoned; to Lodge he angrily concluded that the "clamor of the peace faction has convinced me that this country needs a war."

Roosevelt's view of world power was frankly racist, though idealistic and realistic too. It was in the "interest of civilization," he wrote in 1896, that Britain should assume a dominant role in South Africa, for the efficient English-speaking peoples were in the forefront of orderly human progress. For the same reason, "the United States themselves, the greatest branch of the English-speaking race, should be dominant in the Western Hemisphere." America would do its part to uplift backward peoples if the peace faction didn't "bring this country down to the Chinese level" and erode "the great fighting features of our race." Americans should assume the burden in this hemisphere in Cuba, where a decadent Spanish colonialism was taking more desperate measures to suppress native rebellion. "We ought to drive the Spaniards out of Cuba," Theodore informed Bye in March 1896, "and it would be a good thing, in more ways than one, to do it."

Involvement in Cuba would have produced the ships and defenses that Roosevelt still considered so vital when, a year later, he took over as Assistant Secretary of

1897

the Navy. Fear lest the navy be unprepared made him determined to promote the fleet's effectiveness. With customary zeal he familiarized himself with all operations, afloat and ashore; he identified the ablest officers and the worst administrative methods, investigated every item of equipment from guns to drydocks, studied ways to improve firepower, tactics, strategy. With considerable skill he prodded a hesitant administration and an economy-minded, patronage-preoccupied Congress toward larger appropriations.

McKinley had expressed reservations to Lodge about appointing so energetic a man Assistant Secretary, and Roosevelt admitted that politicians thought him "headstrong, impractical and insubordinate," but he vowed "to be very careful not to let the Sec'y think I am presuming on my position and interfering with him." For the most part he kept that resolve, made more tolerable because Long allowed him considerable leeway, even leaving him in charge in Washington for long periods. Yet Roosevelt could not pass up opportunities at the Naval War College in June and before the Ohio Naval Militia in July 1897 to plump for preparedness. Thereafter, Roosevelt continued tactfully but firmly to press his cautious chief to support increased appropriations and improved planning. If war came, Roosevelt argued, the nation would expect the navy to be ready.

It was in this pattern of careful preparation that Roosevelt, ten days after an explosion sank the *U.S.S. Maine* in February 1898 in Havana harbor, cabled Commodore George Dewey to order the four-cruiser Pacific squadron to Hong Kong, to coal up, and in the event of war "to see that the Spanish squadron does not leave the Asiatic coast, and then [to conduct] offensive operations in the Philippine Islands." Long was shocked when he learned of this order, but he did not countermand it. Actually it was a sensible precaution which Roosevelt had outlined to the Secretary a month before the *Maine* went down. Certainly Roosevelt was a jingo who welcomed war with Spain, but he was also a capable Assistant Secretary who served the Navy and the country well; when McKinley finally yielded in early April to the popular demand for a war declaration, the Spanish squadron in the Philippines did not escape from Dewey.

Roosevelt was one of the few leaders in either party who by 1898 appreciated the realities of power in foreign affairs. He was not without idealism, but he respected facts and recognized strength. He liked to compare statistics on gunfire with his friend Baron Hermann Speck von Sternberg, the German diplomat. He liked to appraise the potential of the world's great nations with charming Cecil Arthur Spring Rice, secretary of the British delegation at Washington. Japan's designs on Hawaii worried Roosevelt, yet he thought that if the Japanese "can stand the strain financially . . . they will be a formidable counterpoise to Russia in the Far East." The Kaiser's designs in Latin America gave concern also; Germany would be wiser to look toward "Russia against her flank and year by year increasing in relative power." In foreign policy, as in domestic, Roosevelt never tired of saying that "I always hate words unless they mean blows."

Eager to get into combat and impatient at delays and

inept administration, devoted to the interests of his men and courageous under fire, Colonel Roosevelt put himself wholeheartedly into the war. He went into an army volunteer unit: that acquainted him with another service under actual field conditions, yet on a less disciplined level that suited his informal methods. He attacked the War Department's mismanagement of the Cuban expedition: that involved him in controversy and perhaps ruled out the Medal of Honor he thought he had earned. He exulted at battle casualties and boasted of his own exploits: that revealed a primitive pride in the savage that was part of Roosevelt and his age. As second in command of the Rough Riders, Roosevelt was an inspiring leader of men.

A more challenging test of leadership awaited him as governor. He had never assumed so much responsibility for governmental operations nor undertaken to work so closely with the machine leaders. Since his early years in the assembly Roosevelt had not dealt closely with the complex problems of urban-industrial society. Chief executive of the largest and most diverse state in the Union, he could not have found a better testing ground, short of the White House, for all his ideas and abilities.

The method by which he tackled the task was crucial. He consulted openly and frequently with Boss Platt, but at the same time insisted upon his right to seek advice from leading independent Republicans. To a degree that he had not found necessary previously, he also solicited the counsel of experts in taxation, canal improvements, labor, schools, and conservation. And he made much greater use of the press, chiefly through daily news conferences, to get advance reaction to proposals and to put his own views before the people.

Carefully picking his way between the machine's wishes and the independents' demands, the governor concentrated first upon political reforms. With Platt's concurrence the legislature replaced the "starchless" civil service regulations with a new law. With the boss's more reluctant approval, Roosevelt also attacked corruption and inefficiency in canal operations by appointing a new superintendent of public works "much above the level of excellence," the press generally agreed, "to which we have become accustomed under partisan and machine governors." For a time Roosevelt in turn supported Platt's schemes to reorganize the administration of the New York City police, but always with the thought of getting the police out of politics; he was relieved when senate opposition frustrated these designs, which many independent Republicans regarded as purely partisan.

The most severe political test of his determination arose over his refusal to reappoint ex-lobbyist and spoilsman Lou Payn, an influential party lieutenant, as superintendent of insurance. Platt opposed this action, as did the insurance company executives, many of whom feared that the governor would not be able to muster enough votes in the senate, but Roosevelt doggedly persisted; he found a good candidate willing to stand, and set about drumming up Democratic support. That effort probably would have fallen short had not a disgruntled stockholder come to the governor with evidence that Payn had borrowed $435,000 upon insufficient collateral from a trust company closely associated in the past with a bonding and surety firm under the superintendent's jurisdiction. Roosevelt handled the ensuing investigation circumspectly, but at last he had a weapon that commanded respect. He proposed to Platt an "honest compromise" upon some organization Republican who would be upright and efficient; and Platt finally agreed to such a man, a Syracuse banker who "for business reasons" had turned down Roosevelt's earlier offer of the same office.

"I have won out," Roosevelt wrote, "by dint of combining inflexible determination with extreme good nature, and resolutely refusing the advice . . . to quarrel with the machine, in which case I should have had about six votes out of fifty in the Senate." "To have compelled the machine to support the best man proposed because it was powerless to aid any poorer candidate," concluded *The New York Times*, "is a triumph for the Governor and the cause of clean politics." "I have always been fond of the West African proverb," the governor added, " 'Speak softly and carry a big stick; you will go far.' "

Legislation affecting corporations presented a different challenge. Here Roosevelt lacked experience; his only program was to seek "the just middle," approaching each issue as an honest broker. Where two powerful streetcar companies were fighting over the Amsterdam Avenue route in New York City, he intervened enough to insure that the public would only have to cross two tracks. When bills granting valuable rights to the Long

Island Railroad, the Consolidated Gas Company, and the rapid transit commissioners were accused of being "grabs" for power Roosevelt insisted upon limitations upon these privileges of fifty years, renewable for twenty-five years; he also adopted the suggestion of Platt's state chairman, that there be "a general tax on franchises."

A bill to tax franchises as real estate happened to be before the legislature, and, despite Platt's opposition, Roosevelt supported it. Indeed, when the machine leaders tried to forestall any action by promoting a rival measure, the governor boldly pushed the real-estate version through. The boss didn't like the beating — no politician who ran his organization with the backing of big business firms would — but an amendment enabled him to save face.

Roosevelt's course on the franchise-tax bill was really a series of pragmatic adjustments to pressures on either hand, but he developed a rational justification. On principle, he contended, corporations enjoying valuable privileges should assume their just share of public burdens. They should accept reasonable imposts also out of expediency, the better to counter drastic and unwise demands. And when the "arrogant public and semi-public corporations" interfered as brazenly as these had against the franchise tax, they had to be set right: "in their own interests," the governor declared, "we must insist that they are the servants and not the masters of the state." His argument amounted to a matured formula for political action; it offered the party of property a way to move forward responsibly in an era of great change.

Roosevelt's old concern about "the wealthy criminal class" that endangered all property through its abuses found expression in the antitrust section of his annual message of January 1900. Agitation against monopoly had risen to the point where Roosevelt thought this the most dangerous domestic issue confronting party and nation, an issue on which an ambitious yet responsible leader in a major state that had just passed a franchise-tax law had to take a stand. As early as August 1899 he began to work out his own position, consulting first informed Republicans, then trying out initial ideas on an Ohio campaign audience, and finally sending a draft of his message to several experts before submitting it to Platt. Out of all this came a statement that condemned the immoral ways in which some men had acquired great wealth and recommended that the state curb such practices by requiring greater publicity of corporate affairs. A bill to this effect never passed either house, and New York corporations continued to report annually only the amounts of their assets, debts, and capital stock with proportion issued. But the exercise developed Roosevelt's eventual position on trusts as President and underscored the importance of public pressure to any realistic reform effort.

Though careful not to minimize the dangers of state intervention in the "delicate and complicated" machinery of business, Roosevelt had continued to adjust his labor policies to experience. The writings of his friend Jacob A. Riis had helped him see how much needed to be done "towards giving a better chance for respectability and usefulness to the people in the crowded lower wards." As police commissioner he learned at first hand about conditions on New York's East Side. By 1897 he shared Riis's optimism that the lot of the workingman was slowly improving, but "if there is going to be any solution of the big social problems of the day," Roosevelt wrote, "it will come, not through a vague sentimental philanthropy, and still less through a sentimental parlor socialism, but through actually taking hold of what is to be done and working, right in the mire." His own party would have "to take hold of the very things which give Tammany its success, and show ourselves just as efficient as Tammany; only, efficient for decency."

As governor, Roosevelt approved bills to increase the power of the factory inspectors, to license sweatshops more rigorously, and to regulate the hours of drug clerks and of employees on state work. He sought without success to put through an employer's liability law. He made some headway in improving enforcement of the labor law, even staging an expedition with Riis to check on East Side conditions. "All I want to do is cautiously feel my way to see if we cannot make the general conditions of life a little easier," he explained to critics, "a little better."

Unions and especially strikes still antagonized Roosevelt, but not as much as they had earlier. Unions encouraged class divisions at the cost of "that capacity for steady, individual self help which is the glory of every true American," but he consulted with labor leaders and appointed Republicans in several crafts to important state positions. Strikes threatened lives and property; he had condemned the Haymarket rioters in 1886, commended Cleveland's handling of the Pullman strike in 1894, and defended strikebreaking cabbies in 1897. Yet as police commissioner he had pledged his help in enforcing municipal hours-and-wages laws and as governor he tried through the state mediation board to settle disputes peaceably. He ordered out the national guard only once, at the request of the sheriff of Westchester County to assist deputies in restraining 750 Italian laborers who had seized the half-finished dam at Croton Reservoir. Even then Roosevelt pursued the investigation of whether the employers were violating the eight-hour law, only to admit finally that "we are powerless to make the contractors give larger wages, though I personally think the wages are too low." Roosevelt as a mediator took a harder line toward laboringmen than he did toward employers, but he moved further toward a just balance than most leaders in either party. He sought a state that would see to it that capital *and* labor got a square deal.

The state should be neutral toward contending factions; it should also be positive in promoting the general welfare. When the special committee he had appointed came out in favor of enlarging the Erie into a 1000-ton barge canal that would serve as a "natural regulator" of freight rates, Roosevelt endorsed that proposal. The first step in "this stupendous undertaking" (eventually completed during World War I) was to pass a $200,000 appropriation for a survey, and though Platt was reluctant to offend anti-canal Republicans in upstate communities in an election year, he finally cooperated with

Roosevelt and the mercantile interests of New York City and Buffalo to put it through.

The governor promoted the general welfare socially as well. He supported successful reform moves to eliminate prize fighting (which he artfully distinguished from boxing) and to establish a tenement house commission. He cooperated closely with educator Nicholas Murray Butler to raise teachers' salaries and put the public schools of New York City "upon a thoroughly efficient basis and absolutely removed from the domain of politics." He advanced the preservation of the Palisades, endorsed protection of municipal water supplies, and reformed the forest, fish and game commission chiefly to effect plans by Chief Forester of the United States Gifford Pinchot for scientific conservation of the Adirondack reserves.

The unanimity with which the independent Republican press supported his renomination was the best testament to the success of his political apprenticeship in the Empire State. He had not accomplished all he desired, but through astute maneuver and careful compromise he had avoided a party fight while carrying his essential point four times out of five. In a most demanding school, Roosevelt had passed the test of leadership. He had developed a mature grasp of the mechanics of political power. He had worked out a philosophy and a program by which his party could attack the great domestic problems of the day. He was prepared for the twentieth century.

IV
"Cautiously but Steadily"
1900-1904

WORD THAT McKinley was dying had reached
Roosevelt on a climb of Mount Marcy in the Adirondacks; a day later, on Saturday afternoon, September 14,
1901, before most of the cabinet in Ansley Wilcox's Buffalo home, Theodore Roosevelt took the oath of office
as the twenty-fifth President of the United States.

Horrified at the anarchist's deed, and anxiously hopeful that McKinley would recover, the American people
had been unsettled for a week. The assurance that things
were not to be changed and that the administration
would remain conservative would "take a weight off the
public mind," the new President learned from his
brother-in-law in New York City. With Secretary of War
Elihu Root beside him, Roosevelt needed no further
urging from the business world. "I wish to say that it
shall be my aim to continue, absolutely unbroken," declared the Chief Executive, "the policy of President Mc-
Kinley for the peace, the prosperity, and the honor of
our beloved country."

That pledge reassured a nation that in November

1900 had strongly endorsed McKinley's policy of prosperity at home and prestige abroad. And through the next three years Roosevelt was only too conscious that he was filling out another's term. But though he moved cautiously, he did so more with an eye to 1904 than 1900. He had to be conservative enough to keep the party's powerful standpatters from promoting Mark Hanna as a more legitimate successor. At the same time he had to be progressive enough to keep those dissatisfied with industrial conditions and eager for greater federal intervention from going over to the Bryan Democrats. Even McKinley had shown some interest in combatting trusts, and more in lowering tariffs through reciprocity agreements; Roosevelt would move in the same direction in a steadier fashion — and would accomplish something.

ROOSEVELT was no stranger to the role as McKinley's shadow; in the campaign of 1900 and as Vice-President he played a secondary part. McKinley conducted a dignified canvass from his front porch in Canton, Ohio, while Roosevelt, under Hanna's direction, crossed the country defending the administration. Once elected to his "utterly anomalous office," Roosevelt found that his chief did not want him "to take any part in affairs or give him any advice." The special session at which he presided over the Senate lasted less than a week; his one major patronage recommendation was ignored. Almost in desperation at having "taken the veil," the Vice-President explored the possibility of resuming law studies so that he might pass the bar exams before 1904.

The uselessness of his position did provide needed time with his family. Since 1889 he had been too busy at public affairs for enough moments with his children; he had made up for it by returning home with large bundles of toys and by concentrating upon their doings when with them. He had his father's gift of total involvement, but the pace was hectic; the games of "bear" before bed often ended in a bumped head. Alice rebelled against him, and he pressed Theodore, Jr., so hard that in 1898 the boy only escaped a minor nervous breakdown by being sent off to join Alice at Auntie Bye's in New York City. "The fact is that the little fellow, who is peculiarly dear to me, has bidden fair to be all the things I would like to have been and wasn't," Roosevelt confessed to the family physician, "and it has been a great temptation to push him."

By 1901 young Ted was at Groton, where his father wrote him regularly; that summer they had time for a week's shooting expedition around Long Island bays. There was leisure, too, for watching Alice ride bareback; for reading *Tales of a Wayside Inn* to Kermit and Ethel, "absorbed in their garden, chickens and guinea pigs"; for romps with seven-year-old Archie, "the sweetest little fellow imaginable," and three-year-old Quentin, that "small boisterous person [who] was in fearful disgrace this morning, having flung a block at his mother's head."

"I am rather ashamed to say that I am enjoying the perfect ease of my life at present," Theodore wrote from Sagamore Hill in April. "I am just living out in the country, doing nothing but ride and row with Mrs. Roosevelt, and walk and play with the children; chop trees in the afternoon and read books by a wood fire in the evening."

But even as he relaxed, political ambition stirred. The campaign of 1900, ironically, had focussed national attention more upon Roosevelt than McKinley; as Finley Peter Dunne's Mr. Dooley remarked, "Tis Tiddy alone that's runnin', an' he ain't r'runnin', he's gallopin'." In January 1901 William Howard Taft had "no doubt that you will be the nominee in 1904," but Roosevelt refrained from speculating upon his chances until after McKinley in June renounced any intention of seeking a third term. Even then the Vice-President treated the prospect lightly, because "the only certain feature of the situation is that my own State will be against me . . . and if the west refuses to take New York's candidate, I think it unlikely that it will take any but a western man."

His trip in August 1901 to the Rough Rider reunion left Roosevelt "greatly astonished at the feeling displayed" for him, not only in Colorado and Kansas, but in Missouri and Illinois. Genuine popular movements in his behalf were influencing G.O.P. leaders there. And if the West was for him, machine opposition in New York would not be so important. In late August Roosevelt began to treat Kansas editor William Allen White as his campaign manager west of the Mississippi. The Vice-

President also looked forward to a fall trip into the South, at Booker T. Washington's invitation to speak at Tuskegee Institute, to attract followers in that vital quarter.

McKinley's death broadened Roosevelt's power. The organization constructed so carefully for McKinley was still intact and presumably responsive to its builder, Mark Hanna, but by astute appointments the new President hoped to bring it gradually over to his side. Roosevelt wanted to come to power in 1904 "in his own right." Quite naturally he turned for help to White, Washington, and others within his fledgling movement. "I must see you as soon as possible," he wrote Washington on September 14; "I want to talk over the question of possible future appointments in the south exactly on the lines of our last conversation together."

His first major appointment in the South showed his intended line. The United States District Judge in Alabama died in October; at once Roosevelt decided to replace him with a Confederate major and former Governor who was a Gold Democrat. The President avoided the radical agrarian Democrats whom he had always opposed and whom Washington distrusted for exploiting racial prejudice. He also avoided the regular Republican organization, which favored a "lily-white" party and was strongly pro-Hanna. Roosevelt was cautious enough usually to leave McKinley Republicans in office until their terms expired, but he sought with Washington's aid to recognize deserving Negroes and to undermine the McKinley-Hanna organization.

steadily he resisted efforts to tone the mes-

s message carefully noted that large cor-
ere a "natural" outgrowth and had contrib-
to America's progress. But they entailed
rave evils" which the federal government
inate. The initial step should be to require
mpanies to reveal more information on their
rther steps to curb abuses were then neces-
uld be planned intelligently.

was not disposed to take up this proposal.
e President have an effective weapon he could
pendently. The Sherman Act of 1890 had out-
binations in restraint of trade, but the Su-
urt had drastically limited its use by ruling
hat "manufacture" did not constitute "com-
here had been only a few federal proceedings
sts, launched by zealous district attorneys in
the Department of Justice had initiated action
Sherman Act solely against labor unions. The
orld betrayed no uneasiness when the attorney-
f Minnesota filed suit in January 1902 against
combination of western railroads just effected
Morgan in the $400,000,000 Northern Securities
.

is spectacular merger of E. H. Harriman's Union
ith James J. Hill's northern roads to control
port in the Northwest made an inviting target.
Street the Northern Securities Company was
proof that combination, not competition, was the

In Southern appointments the President relied also upon skilled Harrison Republicans like Henry C. Payne of Wisconsin (appointed Postmaster General over objections from Robert M. La Follette's faction) and Iowan James S. Clarkson (named surveyor of the port of New York over reform protests). But the invitation to Booker T. Washington for dinner at the White House in October 1901 most irritated Southerners. Roosevelt was an outspoken defender of the colored man's right to equal treatment, and the violent reaction did not keep him from consulting the Tuskegee educator thereafter, or from having Negro federal officials to White House receptions. But the President issued no further dinner invitations to colored men.

Negroes and Democrats did not complicate Roosevelt's effort to take party control in the North. In Colorado, Kansas, and Missouri he personally put his followers into federal office; elsewhere in the Middle West he relied chiefly upon the manipulations of Payne and Clarkson. East of the Alleghenies, where Hanna had never been as strong, Roosevelt was fairly certain of New England; key appointments and judicious cooperation with Senator Quay gained Pennsylvania and New York. As early as 1902 the results began to show in resolutions of state conventions endorsing Roosevelt's renomination. By 1903 the only remaining obstacle was Hanna's refusal to declare himself.

Hanna knew what was happening, but Roosevelt continued to consult him and the two never clashed openly. The President quickly bridled at charges that his appointment policy aimed at his own nomination. He argued that he was trying to treat the races alike, and that it was only wise to put in Gold Democrats, who might side with the Republicans. The men named to office, moreover, were not only capable, but more likely to support the new President's policies. He had many reasons, in short; but however unconsciously, he also had 1904 in mind.

The more demanding task was to fashion a program which would keep the party united while winning the allegiance of the people. Such a program could not be too radical or too conservative. As always, Roosevelt sought a middle ground.

The conservative influences were many and potent. He was pledged to carry on in place of McKinley, and if he estranged standpatters they would gravitate naturally to Hanna. Roosevelt had to reckon with a Congress dominated by safe Republican majorities imbued with *laissez-faire* ideas. Guardians of the great corporations were especially powerful in the Senate, where the Big Four led by traction magnate Nelson W. Aldrich of Rhode Island controlled the important committees. The House of Representatives was not as formidable, but in December 1902 it elected as Speaker Joseph G. Cannon of Pennsylvania, a staunch high-tariff advocate who would rule that chamber until 1910.

Yet pressures for change were also rising. Fires of the Populist revolt had subsided with rising prosperity after 1896, but grievances against railroads and monopolies smoldered among southern and western farmers. Bryan had fanned this dissatisfaction in 1900; in Wisconsin,

Governor La Follette had adde   but
where protests of the 1880's sti.   n.
ers, the middle classes had reco   elt
enough to support municipal an   w
na's Ohio, Toledo had elected S   ch
Jones mayor in 1897; by 1901 the
ington Gladden and single-taxer   m
were fighting utility interests in C   c
land. In 1902 Mayor Johnson woul   f
to the state capital.

Roosevelt had responded to simila
York; on trips west he had kept abre
unrest. He had not shown interest in L
power, but when Albert B. Cummins
Guard's candidate for the gubernatori
Iowa in 1901, the Vice-President had v
in the campaign. "Ever since I met you
that you were the type of man who for
country ought to be high in public life,'
this advocate of railroad regulation and

Convinced that the G.O.P. had to r
trust agitation, the new President balked
from financier J. Pierpont Morgan's repr
his first annual message "say nothing exc
"I intend to be most conservative," he wr
interests of the big corporations themselve
in the interest of the country I intend t
tiously but steadily, the course to which I
licly committed again and again, and whic
is the right course." Cautiously he consu

life of trade; to the West it was the dread portent of higher rates and greater discrimination to come; to Roosevelt it was the logical point of attack. Without consulting anyone other than Attorney-General Knox, the President directed in February 1902 that the Justice Department invoke the Sherman Act against Morgan's newest creation.

Three days after the stock market tumbled at the news, the great financier was in Washington to see the President. "If we have done anything wrong," Roosevelt recalled Morgan asserting, "send your man to my man and they can fix it up." Roosevelt replied that that would be impossible; Knox added that the aim of the suit was not to "fix up" anything but to stop illegal combinations. Organizer of the United States Steel Company and other combines, Morgan asked if the administration would attack his other interests, to which Roosevelt replied "Certainly not . . . unless we find . . . they have done something that we regard as wrong." Morgan "could not help regarding me as a big rival operator," Roosevelt remarked afterwards, "who either intended to ruin all his interests or else could be induced to come to an agreement to ruin none." Roosevelt's stand was unprecedented. He had broken with "the McKinley nexus" to assert the federal government's power against the arrogant captains of finance.

The Supreme Court would break new ground itself by upholding the government's case by a five-to-four decision in 1904, but Roosevelt turned at once to drumming up support for his program of publicity. In April 1902 the administration instituted a similar suit against the "Beef Trust" of Swift and Company. And on a late-summer swing through the northeast the President hammered away at the need to "Destroy the Evil in Trusts, But not Prosperity." There was no cure-all for the trust problem, but the men of great wealth who denied that evils existed were foolish. "I am so far from being against property, when I ask that the question of the trust be taken up," he reassured an enthusiastic Boston audience, "that I am acting, in the most conservative sense, in property's interest."

The fall elections of 1902 appeared to endorse the President's policy, as the Bryan wing of the Democracy made a poor showing and the Republicans captured at least a plurality of the congressional vote in every state outside Nevada and the South. In January 1903 the administration submitted its major recommendations: to enjoin and punish discriminatory rebates in interstate commerce (embodied with the railroads' approval in the Elkins Act), to expedite circuit-court action on antitrust cases (also passed), and to set up a federal agency to aid in carrying out the Sherman Act by requiring reports from large interstate corporations. The Congress finally enacted this last proposal as an amendment (sponsored by Senator Knute Nelson of Minnesota) to the bill creating the Department of Commerce and Labor; a Bureau of Corporations would be formed within that Department to implement Roosevelt's demand.

The Nelson amendment was not as stringent as House Democrats wanted, or as Representative Littlefield of

Maine advocated in his bill to compel companies thereafter organized to submit annual reports to the federal
government. But though Roosevelt was cautious about
this first step, he was steady in insisting, over powerful
protests, on some effective action. Aldrich and other conservatives did not fight long or openly against the President, but they did resist, and they could have defeated
a measure more radically inspired and less skillfully
managed.

The threat to keep Congress in Washington if a suitable
bill did not pass before the regular session expired in
March had been Roosevelt's best weapon initially. A
better one fortuitously appeared when a number of
legislators received telegrams from a Standard Oil executive opposing the Nelson amendment as "an engine
for vexatious attacks against a few large corporations."
In revealing the existence of these messages to the press,
the President incorrectly identified the sender as John
D. Rockefeller, but that astute error dramatized the fact
that the nation's greatest trust was bringing pressure
upon Congress. By a vote of 251 to 10 the House quickly
passed the Nelson-amended conference report over
which it had been quarreling with the Senate. The upper
chamber went along, at the cost of a pledge from Roosevelt to Aldrich, made public by Knox, that "Congress
has now enacted all that is practicable and all that is
desirable."

In selecting heads for the new Department and its
Bureau Roosevelt carefully chose "trained administra-
tors, well known to hold the scales exactly even in all

matters such as those that will come before them." But in locking up the antitrust armory until after 1904, he was more solicitous of the conservatives he had affronted. To help them save face, he gave them more credit than they deserved, telling Taft that it was "far more satisfactory" to work with Hanna and Aldrich "than to try to work with the radical 'reformers,' like Littlefield." Characteristically, Roosevelt gave too little credit to those left of center.

Many antitrust spokesmen regarded the tariff as the "mother of trusts," but Roosevelt found no large body of agreement on the items to be affected, and no item that did not have its defenders. His experience with Cuban reciprocity illustrated the difficulties. Western beet sugar interests opposing concessions to the Cuban raw product secured an amendment removing the differential duty on refined sugar also, whereupon the eastern refiners joined them to defeat the bill in 1902. The next year the President came out strongly for reciprocity again, arguing that the United States had inherited a moral responsibility to succor the ailing economy of that liberated island, but it took an extra session before enabling legislation passed in November 1903. A similar measure for the Philippines did not get through; it was no wonder that Roosevelt put off any deeper involvement in tariff revision until after 1904.

He could not avoid tangling with the other great issue on the domestic economic front — labor. For in the spring of 1902 the United Mine Workers launched a strike against the anthracite mines that soon aroused nationwide concern. In 1900 Mark Hanna had talked the operators into granting a 10 per cent pay increase to striking anthracite miners newly organized by the UMW's young president, John Mitchell, but that settlement had left both sides dissatisfied. Renewing his demands for higher wages, an eight-hour day, and other benefits in 1902, Mitchell appealed for support to the National Civic Federation, a body of prominent industrialists, unionists, and public-spirited citizens founded in 1900 to bring together "reasonable" leaders of industry and labor to settle differences by conference. Federation appeals failed to budge the Reading's arch conservative George F. Baer and his fellow presidents. In May almost all the hard-coal miners walked out.

Relying upon public sentiment to build up against the union, the operators made only a few moves to employ strikebreakers. Mitchell was conciliatory, offering again and again to arbitrate, but George Baer foolishly replied to a suggestion that it was his "religious duty" to end the strike by declaring that "the rights and interests of the laboring men will be protected and cared for — not by the labor agitators, but by the Christian men to whom God in his infinite wisdom has given control of the property interests of this country." Promptly seconded by the Lackawanna's president, Baer's widely circulated remarks undercut the legitimate case of the companies in this already sick industry; despite middle-class fears of union power, the public leaned to the laboringmen's support.

Having investigated the dispute through his Labor

Commissioner, Roosevelt began in August to put pressure upon the operators to compromise. The coal owners however were determined "to do away with what they regard as the damage done to them by submitting to interference for political reasons in 1900." And since Roosevelt had never granted them favors, he had no warrant for a "private or special appeal to them." Other means failing, he was prepared to intervene directly. On October 1, 1902, with the elections only a month away, the President summoned parties to the dispute to confer with him in Washington.

At the conference Mitchell responded to Roosevelt's plea for a settlement by agreeing to submit the case to an arbitral body appointed by the President, provided the verdict would be binding. But the mine officials heatedly rejected talks or arbitration, and refused to recognize the union "outlaws." Instead they called upon the federal government for a court injunction against the strikers, a suit against the union under the Sherman Act, and the use of the army to restore order. They refused even to consider Mitchell's "eminently fair" proposition and "used insolent and abusive language about him," Roosevelt wrote afterwards, "and in at least two cases assumed an attitude toward me which was one of insolence."

The failure of the conference left Roosevelt angry with the operators. Determined to resolve the crisis, he planned to appoint Grover Cleveland and three other eminent leaders to an investigating commission. He also decided to send in federal troops, if necessary, to take over operation of the mines. "I do not know whether I would have had any precedents," he later observed, "but in my judgment it would have been imperative to act, precedent or no precedent — and I was in readiness."

Informed of the President's plans through Elihu Root and J. P. Morgan, the coal executives finally agreed to arbitrate if the panel consisted of an army engineer, a mining engineer, a federal judge, a businessman familiar with the industry, and an "eminent . . . sociologist." By leaving no place for a union representative this prescription stalled negotiations until Roosevelt hit upon the stratagem of naming a trade unionist as the "sociologist." Thereby the companies avoided recognition, the UMW obtained a voice, and Roosevelt sighed in "intense relief." The miners went back to work.

The Anthracite Coal Strike Commission eventually awarded something to each side. The workers received a 10 per cent wage boost and a reduction in hours, but the old method of weighing coal was not changed and a 10 per cent increase in prices was authorized. The companies were not required to recognize the union formally, but the UMW did obtain representation upon an anthracite board of conciliation. All in all, the settlement bore out Roosevelt's contention that he sought a "square deal" for both capital and labor.

Mitchell's exemplary conduct and the operators' "arrogant stupidity" had helped Roosevelt maintain his balance throughout the crisis, yet his patience and skill won editorial acclaim. He had set important precedents in calling the disputing parties to Washington, in naming an arbitral board whose decision was binding, and in planning to seize a great industry.

Fear of social revolution had animated him more than

concern for the miners' condition, but his mission was to bring standpatters to accept reasonable change. That objective reflected a basic concern with national unity in the hazardous adjustment to modern industrial life. Capital and labor had to work together; otherwise the state would remind them of the public interest, by intervening as drastically as need be.

The Constitution set limits which he might have exceeded in taking over the mines. But Roosevelt knew that that document had always been subject to interpretation. Presidents and courts taking a Jeffersonian stand had interpreted federal powers narrowly, as conservatives did in opposing business regulation. Those taking a Hamiltonian view, on the other hand, had interpreted federal powers broadly, as Roosevelt thought any strong executive should. In this attitude he revealed not only a personal delight in the exercise of power, but upon occasion, an authoritation disregard of legal restraints. Yet the anthracite strike also demonstrated "the fuller truth" that "a great exertion of federal authority was the only feasible means of meeting the challenge of the times."

The balance he had maintained through the 1902 crisis was more difficult to achieve where violence erupted. The next year, during a riotous mine strike in Arizona, he ordered federal troops into the territory at the governor's request, but withdrew them when they were used to cow the workers. In 1903 Roosevelt refused to intervene in Colorado against the Western Federation of Miners; when the mine owners struck back viciously at the union with the aid of state militia, on the other hand, he told the syndicalist Federation he had "neither the power nor right" to interfere. Roosevelt detested the radical principles of the Federation's leaders; it was far easier to work with Mitchell.

The propertied middle class distrusted unions more than trusts, but Roosevelt preserved a moderate position. Believing that big labor was as natural a development as big business, he defended the right of workingmen to associate. Believing at the same time in maintaining individual self-help, he defended the right of workingmen to refuse to join a union and favored the "open shop." He therefore approved of the Anthracite Coal Strike Commission's declaration that "no person shall be refused employment or in any way discriminated against on account of membership or nonmembership in any labor organization."

This declaration greatly disappointed labor leaders. And when the bookbinders in the Government Printing Office managed to get the dismissal of a foreman their union had expelled, the AF of L protested any federal move to take him back. But Roosevelt backed up the Civil Service commission's ruling that the man be reinstated, contending that in employment the government could no more discriminate between union and nonunion than between Protestant and Catholic or Gentile and Jew. The most he would do for the AF of L leaders with whom he conferred at the White House (to the horror of many conservatives) was to note publicly that in this decision he was "dealing purely with the relation of the government to its employees" and that "the laws of

the land . . . differentiate any case in which the government of the United States is a party from all other cases
whatsoever." That enabled Gompers to state that the
President favored the open shop in the Government
Printing Office "because the federal law sustains it and
not because he believes it is preferable to full union labor."

Since the President had explained his "unofficial and
private views" frankly to the AF of L leaders, he knew
Gompers had misrepresented him "chiefly in the way of
suppression of essential truths." Still he let Gompers'
statement pass uncorrected. Roosevelt preferred to avoid
public discussion of this delicate issue. He also wanted to
cooperate with responsible officials like Gompers and
Mitchell. The place to draw the line with unions as with
corporations, he believed, was on conduct. Both were
"necessities in our present industrial system," but
"where, in either one or the other, there develops corruption or mere brutal indifference to the rights of others, and shortsighted refusal to look beyond the moment's gain," he wrote, "then the offender, whether
union or corporation, must be fought."

Roosevelt applied this standard of orderly good conduct in foreign as in domestic affairs. He was more cautious abroad than many had feared he would be, but he
steadily pursued the imperial policy of promoting American commerce through overseas bases, a great navy, and
an interocean canal. He championed the Monroe Doctrine in the western hemisphere and American rights
wherever challenged. He was too self-righteous, but he
accomplished much by 1904.

In Cuba the Roosevelt adminstration honored the American pledge of liberation, but only after the Cubans accepted limitations upon their sovereignty that made the new republic a virtual protectorate. For the Philippines an act of 1902 provided civil rule with an elective assembly that launched basic reforms to fit the islanders for self-government, but Roosevelt insisted that talk of independence was premature. Under his watchful eye the Navy acquired a potential base for the Far Eastern squadron at Subig Bay; it also leased a site in 1903 at Guantanamo Bay in Cuba. With practiced skill he began to bring the existing fleet to "the highest point of efficiency, both in material and personnel," and to campaign for more battleships.

The chance of hostilities with England had steadily declined since 1895, but the Roosevelt administration removed several remaining obstacles to the *rapprochement*. In an artful exercise in big-stick diplomacy, Roosevelt resolved the dispute with Canada over the Alaskan boundary through an arbitration that awarded the United States almost all it claimed. The British also agreed to full abrogation of the Clayton-Bulwer pact of 1850 providing for joint control and nonfortification of an isthmian canal. With Roosevelt's hearty endorsement, the Senate in December 1901 approved the result of Hay's second negotiation with Lord Pauncefote, giving exclusive rights of fortification and wartime control of such a waterway to the United States.

Venezuela's failure to honor debts due British and German nationals posed a threat to American plans in the vital isthmian area. On first being notified, in December 1901, of Germany's intention to take measures to collect from the Venezuelan dictator Castro, Secretary of State John Hay registered no objection, as long as there was no territorial aggrandizement. Increasingly fearful of German intentions, however, Roosevelt in 1902 initiated a series of moves to strengthen American naval forces in the Caribbean "in case of sudden war." When Germany and Britain finally broke relations with Venezuela in December 1902 and began to bombard and blockade its ports, Roosevelt readied the fleet for action. At the same time he strongly indicated to the German Ambassador the interest of the United States in a peaceful settlement. Convinced that the American President was in earnest, the German government agreed, along with the British, to submit the issue to the Hague Court.

Roosevelt's change of front reflected a growing awareness that what had once been considered permissible under the Monroe Doctrine now was a danger to hemispheric security. And if European powers could not be permitted to keep the order he deemed necessary, that duty logically fell upon the United States. As financial conditions deteriorated in the strife-torn Dominican Republic in 1904, enhancing the danger that Germany or Italy might intervene to collect the large debt owed their nationals, Roosevelt reluctantly assumed this new responsibility.

He cautiously embodied the first specific statement of this corollary to the Monroe Doctrine in a letter which Root read at a dinner in May 1904 celebrating the second anniversary of the Republic of Cuba. On this happy occasion Roosevelt congratulated "not only Cuba but also the United States upon the showing which Cuba has made." He denied that "the United States has any land hunger or entertains any projects as regards other nations, save such as are for their welfare" and contended that any nation that acted decently, kept order, and paid its obligations "need fear no interference from the United States." Only in the next sentence did he firmly state: "Brutal wrongdoing, or an impotence which results in a general loosening of the ties of civilized society, may finally require intervention by some civilized nation, and in the Western Hemisphere the United States cannot ignore this duty."

The next year he would have to back up this threat by taking over the Dominican customs, but he thought it "the simplest common sense" that "if we intend to say 'Hands Off' to the powers of Europe, sooner or later we must keep order ourselves." He failed to understand that men north and especially south of the border could resent his assumptions. Anti-imperialists disliked his condescending attitude toward Latin peoples and challenged his bland assurance that "civilized" powers had a right to intervene in "backward" countries. What Roosevelt interpreted as "duty" they viewed as desire for control. They were not nearly as certain as he was that the United States was more "righteous" than Germany; a policeman was still a policeman.

Roosevelt most exposed himself to their attack in acquiring the site for an interocean canal. Long his fondest dream, this project had moved tantalizingly close to realization in January 1903 with the signature of the Hay-Herran treaty, providing for payment to Colombia of $10,000,000 and an annual rental of $250,000, in return for a license to build a canal through a strip of land five kilometers wide, controlled by the United States except for the cities of Panama and Colon. In March the United States Senate ratified the pact. But the Colombians re-acted violently against Herran's handiwork. They resented the provision permitting American courts in the canal zone and also the stipulation against independent negotiations with the Panama Company, which controlled the rights granted a defunct French concern to build an isthmian canal. If the treaty went into effect the United States would pay this company $40,000,000 for property upon which $260,000,000 had been expended. Colombia coveted a portion of that $40,000,000.

Roosevelt was exasperated. Neither he nor his advisers understood how seriously Colombians took the issue of sovereignty. Herran did not divulge the order he had received from Bogotá, three days after signing, to withhold his signature. Nor did John Hay indicate how much pressure he had exerted at the instance of the Panama Company's American representative, William N. Cromwell. Roosevelt concluded that the Colombian government had negotiated in bad faith; "those contemptible little creatures in Bogotá" were only after more gold.

When the Colombian Senate rejected the treaty in August 1903, Roosevelt could have turned to the alternative route through Nicaragua. Relying upon engineering advice, he continued to prefer the isthmus. By September he was prepared "in some shape or way to interfere when it becomes necessary so as to secure the Panama route without further dealing with the foolish and homicidal corruptionists in Bogotá." One way was to support a revolution in Panama, long restive under Colombian rule and responsive to the Panama Company's agents.

The Roosevelt administration did not actively foment a revolt, but its manifestly sympathetic attitude encouraged the conspirators directed by Cromwell and a wily adventurer, Bunau-Varilla. They knew that American naval units were being sent to the area (where the United States had landed troops six times under the treaty of 1846 with New Granada to "maintain free and uninterrupted transit" of the isthmus). They could surmise that this time the force would not be used, as in effect it had been previously, to help Colombia retain control. That surmise proved correct: American marines landed at Colon on November 4, 1903, and prevented 300 Colombian regulars from crossing the isthmus by railroad to put down the day-old insurrection. In quick order the United States Government recognized the de facto regime, received Bunau-Varilla as minister, and on November 17 concluded a treaty with the Republic of Panama upon essentially the terms negotiated with Colombia.

The President denied complicity with the revolutionists. But in contending that Colombia had no cause for complaint, he clearly depended upon his own standard. To him, Colombia was no better than "a road agent" who "tries to hold up a United States official," who in turn "is quick enough and has nerve enough to wrest his gun [i.e., Panama] from him." Roosevelt therefore had "scant patience with the hysterical sentimentalist who bewails the act on the ground that maybe the road agent did not mean to shoot, and that anyhow the gun was his and should be immediately restored to him." Guided by the same assumptions that shaped his corollary to the Monroe Doctrine, he set up another inviting target for champions of the rights of Latin-American states.

But while Roosevelt was too self-righteous, his critics were too unappreciative of his accomplishment: he had capped his imperial policies with a dramatic deed that rivalled any of his achievements at home. And while he had antagonized anti-imperialists no less than die-hard conservatives, he had kept the bulk of the party and the people behind him. Indeed, as the G.O.P. convention neared, every obstacle to his nomination disappeared. His vigorous prosecution of the Post Office Department frauds chargeable to previous administrations removed the only threat of scandal. His careful work within the organization eliminated his only rival even before the enigmatic Hanna died in February 1904. The Republicans ratified the obvious in June by naming Roosevelt for President with Charles W. Fairbanks of Indiana as his running mate.

The Democrats rejected a Bryanite as their candidate in favor of the conservative Alton B. Parker of New York. But their strategy to attract the Old Guard failed. With Root's aid Roosevelt cultivated the view that his intervention in business was the best insurance against more radical and truly harmful action. The administration also launched no new bolts against the industrial community. When Parker went so far finally as to imply that the Republicans had raised a great campaign fund by virtually blackmailing the great corporations, Roosevelt struck back effectively, branding the charge "a wicked falsehood." He knew that industrialists were contributing, but Parker's implication that the threat of action by the Bureau of Corporations was in any way involved gave the President the opportunity he exploited.

Backed by over $2,000,000 in corporate gifts, the G.O.P.'s national ticket rolled up an electoral majority of 196 and a popular margin of over 2,500,000 votes. The extent of that victory confirmed the appeal of the Square Deal. It endorsed the diplomacy pursued so successfully abroad. It showed that Roosevelt had emerged "in his own right," the most popular American political leader of his time.

V

"The Just Man Armed"
1905-1909

"ON THE fourth of March next I shall have served three and a half years, and this three and a half years constitutes my first term," a grateful Roosevelt told the celebrants at the White House on election night. "The wise custom which limits the President to two terms regards the substance and not the form," he added. "Under no circumstances will I be a candidate for or accept another nomination."

Roosevelt spoke out of conviction. He thought that by 1908 the principles he espoused would fare better under a fresh man "free from the animosities and suspicions which I had accumulated." More important, he recognized the dangers in the great power the President wielded: it was "natural that the people should desire to hedge it about with certain restrictions," he wrote, "and above all to make it certain that it can only be of limited duration."

The power of the President was most extensive in foreign affairs, and wisely so, Roosevelt believed, because the people did not have the steady interest in events abroad that America's position demanded. As long as he was Chief Executive, he intended to supply that vital need. He intended also, where required, to work closely with the Senate, though that body too often became "merely obstructive." In any case, he would promote the national interest as he interpreted it.

Assuming generally the role of "the just man armed," Roosevelt repaired some of the damage caused by canal diplomacy in Latin America. He mediated the Russo-Japanese War and propped up the balance of power in the Far East. He even played a part in resolving the dangerous crisis among European powers over Morocco. His realistic approach to peace raised as many questions as it answered, but at least it acknowledged that America had come of age. Under his leadership, the United States for the first time assumed its responsibilities as a new world power.

─────

In this crucial area Roosevelt was fortunate to have able aides. He had relied heavily at first upon John Hay, whose friendliness toward England had shown to particular advantage in the settlement of the Alaskan boundary dispute. At Hay's death in 1905 the post of Secretary of State went to ex-Secretary of War Elihu Root, who along with William Howard Taft had carried through a difficult negotiation with the Vatican for the transfer to the Filipinos of 400,000 acres of land once held by Spanish friars. Root's patience and tact proved most effective where Hay had been weak, in working with the Senate and improving relations with Latin-American states. And the portly Taft, Root's replacement as Secretary of War, rendered exceptional service in Cuba and the Far East as the administration's troubleshooter.

Roosevelt was intimately involved in diplomacy. On matters of importance he communicated directly with American ministers abroad and even with other heads of state. In Washington he spoke frankly with foreign representatives he trusted; when he did not get along with an embassy chief, he turned to a "kitchen ambassador" like Cecil Arthur Spring Rice (whom the British refused to send to the United States officially) or Speck von Sternberg (appointed head of the German delegation in 1903). Roosevelt was informal, and upon occasion so secretive that observers never realized what he had really done. He was willing to see others receive the credit if that served American interests.

America's imperial course since 1898 had secured the chief objects of "the large policy" in overseas bases and a canal site; the chief task remaining was to preserve the new empire against encroachment or war. Roosevelt assumed that Great Britain would cause no trouble, because her interests were "identical" with America's in the Western Hemisphere and the Orient: "I never even take into account a war with England," he wrote in 1905; "I treat it as out of the question." But he was not so sure about Germany, or about the intentions of Russia and Japan in the Far East, where China's weakness invited further exploitation. If one or more of these great powers endangered the peace in any way that might impinge upon America's farflung interests, Roosevelt could not be indifferent. Indeed, for lack of any international system of guarantees, the United States was obliged to help maintain a balance of power that would restrain aggressive states.

The balance of power varied with the area and the situation, but its success always depended upon responsible action by the nations that stood "at the head of civilization." The United States, one of those nations, should assume its rightful burden within its particular sphere and set an example of how any great country should act within the international order. Toward the weak states under its influence it should be benevolent, treating them fairly while protecting their independence. Toward the strong beyond its special province, on the other hand, it should be graciously firm, giving them no cause for just complaint yet requiring that they do the same.

"I shall try to do exact justice to them; to show them every consideration and courtesy; to ask nothing from them that we should not be willing to grant them in return ourselves," he remarked of his policy toward the Japanese as well as the rest of the world in 1907, "and at the same time to make it evident that in following out this course I am not in the slightest degree influenced by fear of them, and that I will no more permit my country to be wronged than I will sanction its committing wrong in return." "In any event we can hold our own in the future, whether against Japan or Germany, whether on the

Atlantic or the Pacific," he wrote Lodge in June 1905, "only if we occupy the position of the just man armed."

Protected by two oceans, the United States did not require a large standing army, but Roosevelt thought it needed a navy second only to England's. Checking carefully upon top assignments and gunnery results, he had given personal attention to building up efficiency. He had also begun what was to be an almost continual campaign for more ships. Before February 1905, when the House approved two more 16,000-ton battleships of the pre-*Dreadnought* type to cost $7,500,000 each in a $150,-000,000 annual budget, the Congress had authorized construction of eight battleships, six cruisers, and four submarines at Roosevelt's behest. In 1906 and 1907 he was content with only one additional battleship annually of the *Dreadnought* class which England had inaugurated, but concern over Japan's building program caused him to request four such vessels in 1908 (he got two) and two in 1909 (which Congress approved). At the same time he obtained funds for developing a fortified base with dry dock facilities at Pearl Harbor.

Roosevelt pushed ahead the building of the Panama Canal "because it will nearly double the efficiency of our Navy." The seven-man Isthmian Canal Commission set up under the Spooner Act of 1902 to supervise construction was such a cumbersome device that by 1904 work was almost at a standstill; when Congress refused to act, the President by executive order centralized direction, first in a three-man executive committee, and finally in a single chairman. The difficulties in letting contracts to private firms caused further dispute; in February 1907 Roosevelt decided to give the whole job to the army. Placing Major George W. Goethals in full charge, he concluded the administrative reorganization which with few alterations carried the vast work to successful completion in 1914.

Roosevelt continued to play the policeman of the Caribbean. To forestall European intervention, he became deeply involved in Dominican affairs. He also landed troops and set up a provisional government in Cuba to restore order in 1906. When the Venezuelan dictator Castro was unwilling to consider arbitration of claims of injured American citizens in 1908, Roosevelt thought "it would be well to have several ships at once sent there and arrangements made to send a transport with Marines to land." Root's caution prevented such action, but the United States did break off diplomatic relations with Venezuela until Castro was overthrown.

Roosevelt's intervention in Santo Domingo was at least responsible. The financial situation there had continued to deteriorate until the Dominican Republic agreed in February 1905 to a protocol providing for American control of its customs houses. To Roosevelt's immense disgust, the Senate failed to ratify this pact, though an Italian cruiser had appeared to the accompaniment of new protests from French and Belgian creditors. At the request of Dominican officials, therefore, and with prior approval of Senate leaders of both parties, Roosevelt by executive action appointed an American as collector of customs, thereby inaugurating a period of economic progress such as the islanders had never known. He kept this *modus vivendi* in force until Root in 1907 mustered the two-thirds vote needed for Senatorial approval.

Root owed his success in part to his skill at satisfying the solons' pride, in part to the fact that the 1907 treaty reduced both the American obligation and the Dominican compromise of sovereignty. Roosevelt could not admit to having handled the original negotiation poorly; instead he blamed the Senate, which was "such a helpless body when efficient work for good is to be done." But he was particularly pleased to have Root take Hay's place in July 1905 because "I believe he will get on well with the Senate." Roosevelt desired to avoid similar embarrassment in the future.

Under the treaty of 1903 the President already had the right to intervene in Cuba, but in the crisis of 1906 he used that power cautiously. As violence spread Roosevelt dispatched fleet units to Havana and directed Taft to try to re-establish order. Imperialists like Senator Albert J. Beveridge of Indiana urged that the island be seized, while anti-imperialists argued against any action by the United States, but Roosevelt rejected both extremes. When the warring factions could not be reconciled, he approved establishment of an American provisional government to rule until new elections could be held. And in February 1909, to the amazement of many Europeans who had never expected the United States to leave, control of the republic passed to the new President and Congress the Cubans had chosen the previous December.

Roosevelt's notion of "exact justice" did not include arbitration of Colombia's demand for compensation for the loss of Panama, but he backed Root's efforts to improve relations with Bogotá in other ways. With Roosevelt's approval the Secretary of State further cultivated goodwill to the south by his collaboration with Mexico in the Central American Peace Conference of 1907 and by his unprecedented tour of South American capitals in conjunction with the Third Inter-American Conference that convened in 1906 at Rio de Janeiro. "This was the psychological moment for him to go," Roosevelt wrote of Root's trip, "and though in a sense it may truthfully be described, as it has been described, as a sentimental journey, it is one of those journeys of sentiment which are of real importance." In noting afterwards "how well the Pan-American Conference has gone off" Roosevelt was decidedly optimistic. "Root's going there was a great stroke," he told peace advocate Andrew Carnegie. "Gradually we are coming to a condition which will insure permanent peace in the Western Hemisphere."

The statement of the Roosevelt corollary to the Monroe Doctrine clouded that vision for sensitive Latin Americans. Moreover, the encouragement that Root and other officials were beginning to give to American financial interests in the Caribbean area foreshadowed the "dollar diplomacy" that anti-imperialists would condemn in the Taft administration. But consistent with his view of the interest and duty of the United States in this hemisphere, Roosevelt with Root's invaluable counsel had worked for stability and progress. By the standards of the era and of what was possible, he had acted responsibly and well.

The Far Pacific was second in importance only to the

Caribbean in Roosevelt's foreign policy; and on matters
Oriental he took a more decisive role personally. Hay
was so ill at the time that Roosevelt handled the mediation of the Russo-Japanese conflict. He also directed the
intricate maneuvers to maintain a balance of power that
would protect the Philippines, preserve China, and contain Japan. Given the difficult situation, and the inadequate means at his disposal, his realistic approach
achieved a good deal.

Swayed by the call of Duty and Destiny, the American
people had approved annexation of the Philippines.
They had welcomed Hay's notes to the great powers in
1899 and 1900 calling for equality of commercial opportunity in China and the preservation of that country's
territorial integrity. They had even accepted the partici-
pation of American troops in the punitive expedition of
the European states against Peking in 1900, during the
anti-foreign Boxer Rebellion. Yet by and large they did
not appreciate the new responsibilities of imperial America across the Pacific. By March 1901 Roosevelt was la-
menting that "public opinion is dull on the question of
China." He found it dull on the Philippines also, as Congress refused to grant tariff concessions vital to that
agrarian economy. For anything beyond defense of the islands from armed attack, he could not count upon popular support.

In two books published by close friends in 1900, on the
other hand, Roosevelt found a prescription for a positive
policy. Great Britain was declining and Russia rising as a
world power, Brooks Adams argued in *America's Eco-*

nomic Supremacy, so the United States would have to forsake isolation to redress the balance; in China especially, where the Russians were expanding into Manchuria, "America must more or less completely assume the place once held by England." China was critical as well for Alfred T. Mahan, but in his *The Problem of Asia* he pictured a struggle there between the land-based forces of Russia in the north and the sea-based strength of Britain, Germany, Japan, and the United States centered on the Yangtze Valley to the south. Cooperation among these naval powers to control that great commercial valley, Mahan contended, would preserve the "open door" and keep China free of Russian domination.

Roosevelt had not much feared the Russians; he had even admired the "civilizing" influence which their march eastward had exerted upon the "backward" Asians. But as the Tsarist regime betrayed a disposition after 1900 to convert its "exceptional position" in Manchuria into an exclusive preserve, the President became increasingly hostile. England reacted to the threat in 1902 by forming a defensive alliance with Japan; in 1903, Secretary Hay made such a sharp protest over Manchuria that the Russian Ambassador thought the United States might be about to join the Anglo-Japanese entente. Roosevelt and Hay knew that public opinion would not sanction "any scheme of concerted action with England and Japan which would seem openly hostile to Russia," but Hay's stand helped to bring St. Petersburg to agree to evacuate its troops and permit the opening of all Manchurian ports except Harbin. "I think the Russian business is in pretty fair shape," Roosevelt wrote Hay; "I don't intend to give way."

Roosevelt's reversal had its parallel in his attitude toward Japan. Though always respecting the Japanese for their rapid modernization, in the 1890's he had feared their designs in the Pacific. It was only when the United States had satisfied its own territorial ambitions, and the Japanese had seemingly accepted the annexation of Hawaii and the Philippines, that Roosevelt's suspicions yielded to admiration of their efficiency and fighting ability. Moreover, he came to think that they could serve as the natural counterpoise to the Russians. By helping to effect the strategic balance of power that Adams and Mahan had described, Japan could serve American interests in the Far East.

Fearful that Russia might prevail or China somehow be endangered, Roosevelt made some attempt to keep the Russo-Japanese dispute over Korea and Manchuria from deteriorating into war. But when Japan initiated hostilities in February 1904 with a surprise attack upon the Russian fleet at Port Arthur, he was "thoroughly well pleased with the Japanese victory, for Japan is playing our game." If only Japan would not "get the 'big head' and enter into a general career of insolence and aggression," he cautioned Japanese Ambassador Takahira and Baron Kaneko, a Harvard classmate, but "would simply take her place from now on among the great civilized nations," then the island empire had a great future. Conceding that Japan had "a paramount interest in what surrounds the Yellow Sea, just as the United States has a paramount interest in what surrounds the Caribbean," Roosevelt really urged that Japan adopt the model of the just man armed.

Their assurances did not dispel Roosevelt's foreboding that a victorious Japan might become so strong and arrogant as to champion the yellow race against the whites throughout the Far East. Nor did they remove his concern that Japan and Russia might somehow patch up their differences, in league with Germany and/or France, to turn upon England and America. The more he weighed the possibilities, the more he inclined to a settlement that would not favor Japan or Russia unduly, that would preserve a balance between them as the chief basis for stability in the region. When the Russians lost Port Arthur in January 1905, Roosevelt strongly urged them to make peace upon Japan's terms (control of Korea and of the Russian rights at Port Arthur, return of Manchuria to China). He renewed his pressure after Japan's victory at Mukden in March.

By then the war party in Japan was pressing for a money indemnity and for a cession of territory, which the Tsar refused to consider, but Takahira confidentially confessed to Roosevelt that Japanese moderates were anxious for peace. And after administering a crushing defeat to the Russian fleet in May, the Japanese government secretly requested the President "directly and entirely of his own motion and initiative to invite the two belligerents to come together for the purpose of direct negotiation." Carefully concealing this request, Roosevelt with French and German support skillfully brought the Tsar to consent to such a meeting — provided Japan also agreed! Two days later the President publicly invited the two powers to a conference, which finally convened in August 1905 at Portsmouth, New Hampshire.

Officially Roosevelt took no part in the Portsmouth negotiations beyond graciously introducing the delegates aboard the yacht *Mayflower;* behind the scenes, he was most active. At his suggestion the Japanese first advanced their minimal demands in Korea and Manchuria, which with some adjustments the Russians accepted, but the conference threatened to break down over questions of an indemnity and cession of territory. Roosevelt secured the Tsar's assent to relinquish at least the part of Sakhalin Island which Japanese troops had partially occupied. Through appeals that went as high as the Mikado, on the other hand, the President prevailed upon Japan to accept the southern half of Sakhalin in lieu of an indemnity. With that issue resolved, the conferees quickly agreed upon final terms.

Though he acknowledged the contribution of so many others to this difficult settlement, Roosevelt deserved the congratulations that came to him from every quarter. Working practically as his own Secretary of State, he had employed to the fullest his lines of personal communication to every major capital. He had cooperated most closely with Takahira and Kaneko, whose trust in his judgment and good faith had done much to shape Japanese policy. Despite every annoyance over the stubborn pride of the Russians, he had patiently restrained his temper. In a tactful yet realistic manner he had labored to restore a peaceful balance of power.

But Roosevelt had to bear criticism for disappointments felt on either side. Once the Japanese gave up their insistence on a money indemnity, the Tsar thought he had yielded to Roosevelt on Sakhalin too easily. Far more serious, the military faction in Japan charged that the President had deprived their victorious forces of their due. Disturbed at the anti-American demonstrations in Tokyo, Roosevelt suggested to Baron Kaneko "that it would be well for the Japanese to point out, or at least to lay stress on, the enormous amount they have won," but the moderates found it safer to keep silent. In fact, they knew that Japan's resources had been so depleted that the war could not have been long continued, but they could not admit that either. A foreign leader made a convenient scapegoat.

Roosevelt had known enough of Japan's troubles to argue effectively against continuing an expensive war just to gain money or territory. That counsel had helped the moderates in Russia as well as in Japan. It had also promoted Roosevelt's strategy in the Far East. "While Russia's triumph would have been a blow to civilization, her destruction as an eastern Asiatic power would also in my opinion be unfortunate," he had confided to Lodge before Portsmouth. "It is best that she should be left face to face with Japan so that each may have a moderative action on the other."

Japan's spectacular rise to power had left her too insecure to submit to such a balance without assurances beyond the Treaty of Portsmouth. Roosevelt had therefore welcomed the renewal in June 1905 of the Anglo-Japanese alliance. More than that, he was willing to add to

England's his own recognition of Japan's pre-eminent position in Korea. "We can not possibly interfere for the Koreans against Japan," he had told Hay as early as January 1905; "They couldn't strike one blow in their own defence." In July he had confirmed Taft's statement to Premier Katsura in Tokyo that the President was agreeable to Japanese suzerainty over Korea, in return for Japan's promise to leave the Philippines alone. Since this understanding was not embodied in a treaty it would not be binding upon Roosevelt's successors, but both sides recognized that the United States could not engage in a more formal arrangement.

By thus aligning his country secretly with Japan and England Roosevelt stretched the executive power to its limit. In his view, however, the commitment was clearly justified. For Japan's swift rise had also left her too strong to be trusted. The Taft-Katsura agreement would at least protect the Philippines. At the same time it would serve Roosevelt's strategy by turning Japan's development toward the mainland. "So long as Japan takes an interest in Korea, in Manchuria, in China," he wrote Spring Rice in December 1904, "it is Russia which is her natural enemy."

Roosevelt did not foresee that Japan and Russia might come to an agreement (as they did secretly in 1907) upon their exclusive spheres of influence in Korea, Manchuria, and Outer Mongolia. But then by 1907 the realignment of powers in Europe was affecting any "natural" rivalry in the Orient. Having formed an entente with France against Germany, Great Britain by 1907 was drawing closer also to France's ally Russia. The British government thus wanted its Japanese ally to come to some settlement with Russia over North China. The new Russo-Japanese accord modified Britain's strategy for the sake of the more vital European balance.

Not completely privy to this shift in British policy, Roosevelt continued to rely upon the balance of power in North China. He could not have done much more than that. The American people would not intervene to keep the door open for American interests in Manchuria. Nor could China resist Russo-Japanese encroachments successfully.

Roosevelt of course shared the imperialist view that the Chinese were a "backward" people unable to organize their economy efficiently or even to keep order without aid from outside. In this weakened state they were prey to unscrupulous interference. But the anti-foreign movement of the Chinese nationalists seemed to him the wrong remedy. If China was ever to progress, it needed help from abroad to develop transport and industry. And if China was to avoid exploitation, it needed the responsible cooperation of the great powers to maintain equitable opportunities throughout the land. "I will absolutely support the Emperor's policy," Roosevelt instructed the Ambassador to Germany in 1905, "for the preservation of the integrity of China, the open door, and equal rights in China for the commerce of the whole world."

This policy promoted American (and German) interests as well, yet he could not rely upon his own country to enforce it. He would have had even less support if he had done more to encourage the nationalism that young Chinese intellectuals were espousing. When their resentment at American immigration policies threatened to incite a boycott of American goods in 1905, Roosevelt could not yield on the restriction against laborers, but he did try to eliminate discriminatory practices against the professional classes still admissible under the Chinese Exclusion Act. He could not yield either in opposing the anti-American boycott and demonstrations, but after they subsided he did approve the return to China of the Boxer indemnity fund, to be used for scholarships for Chinese students in American universities. Domestic pressures, chiefly in the West and from labor, limited his vision on China as much as his imperialist attitude.

Too persistent in regarding China in colonial terms, Roosevelt was more sensitive to the changes that had come over an industrialized Japan. In the negotiations ending at Portsmouth he had gone to greater lengths than Americans realized to influence Japan to wield its power moderately. He hoped that his own country would respond in kind. "I wish to see the United States treat the Japanese in a spirit of all possible courtesy, and with generosity and justice," he wrote in June 1905. "At the same time I wish to see our navy constantly built up and each ship kept at the highest point of efficiency as a fighting unit." The just man armed, he believed, would have no trouble. "But if we bluster; if we behave rather badly to other nations; if we show that we regard the Japanese as an inferior and alien race, and try to treat them as we have treated the Chinese," he warned, "and if at the same time we fail to keep our navy at the highest point of efficiency and size — then we shall invite disaster."

Agitation against Orientals in California finally produced the incident Roosevelt dreaded when the San Francisco Board of Education in 1906 ordered all ninety-three Japanese, Chinese, and Korean students in the city into a segregated school. Angered at this "wicked absurdity" that aroused such protest across the Pacific, the President assured Baron Kaneko that "I shall exert all the power I have under the Constitution to protect the rights of the Japanese who are here." Roosevelt at once began to put pressure upon the Californians to rescind the order, which the Japanese claimed violated the treaty of 1894 providing mutual guarantees for Americans residing in Japan and Japanese in the United States. At the same time he told the Japanese Ambassador that "in my judgment the only way to prevent constant friction between the United States and Japan was to keep the movement of the citizens of each country into the other restricted as far as possible to students, travelers, businessmen, and the like." Under an immigration agreement of 1900, Japanese laborers were not issued passports to come directly to the United States, but they were still entering through Hawaii. "I earnestly hoped," Roosevelt added, "his Government would stop their coolies, and all their working men, from coming either to the United States or to Hawaii."

Encouraged by the Ambassador's response, Roosevelt proceeded to settle the immediate difficulty while effecting a more permanent solution. At a White House conference in February 1907 a San Franciscan delegation consented to admit aliens of any nationality to nonsegregated schools if they knew English and could enter the proper grade. The President in turn promised to seek to exclude coolies. To do this quietly yet effectively, Root initiated negotiations that Taft concluded in Japan in October 1907 with the "Gentlemen's Agreement," whereby the two countries undertook to limit migration of their nationals to "gentlemen." Despite continued difficulties in enforcement, the influx of Japanese laborers into the United States slowed toward a stop.

But other acts of discrimination against the Japanese in California meantime had built up a dangerous crisis. Some reports coming into the White House from abroad even suggested that Japan was contemplating war. Much as he deplored the foolish insults Californians were perpetrating, Roosevelt did not think these constituted "a shadow of pretext." "If the Japanese attack us now, as the German, English and French authorities evidently think that they will," he wrote Root in July 1907, "it will be nakedly because they wish the Philippines and Hawaii — or, as their heads seem to be swollen to a marvelous degree, it is possible they may wish Alaska." The President did not think they would attack, yet "there is enough uncertainty to make it evident that we should be very much on our guard and should be ready for anything that comes."

While he extended one hand to Japan in friendship, Roosevelt readied the other for combat. Although

smaller in size than the American, Japan's fleet had performed most effectively against Russia and was beginning to acquire the more powerful *Dreadnought*-type
battleship. Moreover, the Japanese navy was concentrated in the Pacific, whereas most of the United States
force was stationed on the Atlantic seaboard. In June
1907 the joint board of army and navy experts recommended that all operational battleships (the fleet, said
Mahan, must never be divided) be dispatched to the Pacific as soon as possible. Thereupon Roosevelt decided,
as he wrote Lodge, that "this winter we shall have
reached the period when it is advisable to send the whole
fleet on a practice cruise around the world." Such a voyage, he reasoned, would afford experience in peace for
what might be required in war. It would have "a pacific
effect" upon the Japanese, who "seem to have about the
same proportion of prize jingo fools that we have." It
would focus attention upon his campaign to get Congress
the next year to authorize not one but four more battleships of the *Dreadnought* class.

Roosevelt hastened to inform the Japanese Ambassador of the "intended trip of the battleship fleet thru the
Pacific," being careful to mention that "it would return
home very shortly after it had been sent out there; at least
in all probability." He also sent Taft on a Far Eastern
tour. The Secretary's report in October 1907 that the
Japanese were in no financial shape for war and "most
anxious to avoid" it was reassuring. Yet the voyage would
dramatize the ability to defend Pacific interests and remind the American people of their commitments as a

world power. Roosevelt especially despaired that their lack of concern made the Philippines "our heel of Achilles" in Asia. "To keep the islands without treating them generously and at the same time without adequately fortifying them and without building up a navy second only to that of Great Britain, would be disastrous in the extreme," he wrote Taft. "Yet there is danger of just this being done."

Reconciled to "a nearly complete independence" for the Philippines "at the earliest possible moment" consistent with their welfare, Roosevelt was determined meantime to defend them. As the fleet moved around South America into the Pacific, he contended so vigorously for four more battleships that Congress in 1908 authorized two — which was all he had really expected. And after the great white ships departed Japan on their way home, Root concluded an exchange of notes with Takahira that enlarged upon the Taft-Katsura accord. In this executive agreement of November 1908 the two nations announced their "common aim, policy, and intention" to maintain the *status quo* in the Pacific and respect each other's possessions there. They would defend the principle of the Open Door in China, and support "by all pacific means . . . the independence and integrity of China."

The Root-Takahira agreement reaffirmed American policy toward China in such broad terms that it has been criticized for giving Japan a free hand in Manchuria. Root did not intend a surrender to Japan on this point. Nor did he and Roosevelt believe that any understanding would restrain an aggressive Japan. Intent upon getting two more battleships from Congress in 1909 (which he did), Roosevelt virtually ignored the Root-Takahira exchange. In fact, he realized that American objectives in Manchuria were beyond American power, but to admit that publicly would only have encouraged Japan and retarded the defense effort he thought necessary in the Pacific. At the risk of misleading the people on America's true position on the Asian continent, the President was committed to a holding action by whatever means.

In this perspective the fleet's voyage around the world served a useful purpose. Yet by revealing weaknesses no less than by brandishing strengths, this parade of naval might aided the militarists in Japan against the moderates Roosevelt favored. The model of "the just man armed" required a balance as delicate as that among the powers in Asia and Europe. It required a responsibility and skill difficult to maintain in the best of times. With inadequate tools, and amid shifting alignments he could not fully understand, Roosevelt had labored to effect a kind of "Square Deal" among the powers in Asia. The wonder was not that he failed in some regards, but that he attained so much.

In the Atlantic, Roosevelt confronted more directly the mounting rivalry among the great nations. And he assumed an even more unprecedented role, for an American President, in composing European differences peaceably.

The trouble that erupted in 1905 over Morocco exposed the developing rivalry. England and France had long been at odds in north Africa, but in 1904, as part of a *rapprochement* against the German threat, they agreed to respective spheres of influence in Egypt and Morocco. The subsequent tightening of the French hold upon the Moroccan Sultanate antagonized Germany, which had its interests and ambitions there under guarantees of equal opportunity dating from a treaty of 1880. In March 1905 the aggressive Emperor Wilhelm II landed from a German warship at Tangier to denounce French interference with the open door in Morocco. His bristling attitude portended war.

In Washington the German Ambassador made "an urgent appeal" that the President find out whether the British "intend to back up France in gobbling Morocco," but Roosevelt regarded any intervention cautiously. "We have other fish to fry and we have no real interest in Morocco," he wrote Taft, and "I do not care to take sides between France and Germany in the matter." Still he was "sincerely anxious to bring about a better state of feeling between England and Germany," who were working up "a condition of desperate hatred of each other from sheer fear of each other." Believing neither intended to attack the other, he authorized Taft to make an "absolutely frank" inquiry that would avoid any suspicion of collusion with Germany. And after Delcassé's fall from power in June 1905 removed the most anti-German influence in the French Government, Roosevelt decided to approach both France and Germany about the Sultan's call for an international conference on Morocco.

As in the concurrent talks ending the Russo-Japanese War, Roosevelt made a good mediator. Fundamentally he sided with France (as he had with Japan), but he was impartial enough to win the Kaiser's confidence (as he had the Tsar's). At the same time he enjoyed as close a relationship with the French Ambassador, Jusserand, with whom he often hiked and played tennis, as with Speck von Sternberg, the German Ambassador. Working intimately with the sympathetic Jusserand, Roosevelt first helped to persuade the French Government to drop its opposition to the Sultan's proposal. He then interceded successfully with Germany to accept a preliminary negotiation with France on an agenda. Speck even informed Roosevelt that in case of any differences arising between the two countries during the conference, the Kaiser "will be ready to back up the decision which you should consider to be the most fair and the most practical." Informed of that promise, the French overcame their remaining doubts.

Roosevelt's part in this negotiation had been secret, but the United States sent Henry White as an official delegate to the conference that convened at Algeciras, Spain, in January 1906. And when a deadlock developed, Roosevelt went so far as to propose a compromise formula reaffirming the open door in Morocco but placing the Sultan's police under French and Spanish supervision. The Kaiser objected to this police organization because it "would be tantamount to a Franco-Spanish double mandate and mean a monopoly of these two countries," but Roosevelt maintained that it was equitable, France having yielded its claim to "organize the police in Moroccan ports through the agency of her officers alone." Reminded of the promise to back up the President's decision — a promise Speck had put more categorically than Wilhelm had realized — the Kaiser finally accepted "the fundamental idea" of "French and Spanish officers to be about equally divided in each of the ports."

Dispatch of a delegate to Algeciras had aroused so much isolationist opposition in America that Henry White had been authorized to state, at the final signing, that the United States disclaimed any political interests in Morocco or responsibility for enforcement of the treaty. Still the Senate was reluctant to ratify the Algeciras convention, and only did so after putting White's statement into a formal reservation. As in the Far East, Roosevelt had taken a greater part in preserving world peace than his country would accept.

For his mediation in the Russo-Japanese War and the Moroccan crisis the President received the Nobel Peace Prize in 1906 — the first American to be so honored. But his further efforts at promoting peace were not so fruitful. American delegates to the Second Hague Conference in 1907 tried unsuccessfully to frame a general arbitration treaty binding on all nations, and to strengthen the Hague Court by making it a permanent body. Roosevelt found even less interest among the European powers in his proposal to limit the building of the *Dreadnought*-type battleships by some international agreement. He correctly foresaw that if such a step was not taken soon, a wholly new race in naval armament would ensue, but rivalry and suspicion were already too great for reasonable discussion. "Altogether," he conceded in February 1907, "the whole subject is full of difficulties."

The Japanese threat dealt the final blow to Roosevelt's hope for a reasonable arms restriction. Indeed, from the summer of 1907 on, he made far more headway at building dreadnoughts than he ever had at limiting them. Having found no alternative to the naval race, he determined that the United States would not fall behind. And he put so much into the contest that he really heightened the rivalry he had often deplored.

Roosevelt continued to trust that the civilized nations would not war on one another, yet he was as convinced as ever of the need for strength to defend liberty at home and secure justice abroad. In flirting with the naval limitation scheme, he had not favored disarmament; the nations "at the head of civilization" needed weapons for defense against "military despotism or barbarism." Moreover, he did not shrink from a war that was justified; he always "put righteousness above peace." "I have fought, not very successfully," he wrote in December 1907, "to make our people understand that unless freedom shows itself compatible with military strength, with national efficiency, it will ultimately have to go to the wall."

Roosevelt saw no alternative to force in the conflict of peoples. Nor did he recognize any arbiter of what was "just," in any major dispute, other than the nation itself. Confident of his own ability to determine "exact justice," he never admitted that there could even be serious question of his views of the world. He never understood that peace-loving men could desire a standard of law less personal, a structure of enforcement less national.

Yet Roosevelt had set a higher standard in foreign re-

lations than prevailed generally in his day. And taking
the world as it was, he had worked skillfully to harmo-
nize conflict into a stability that would serve the best interests of America, and indeed of mankind. Eminently
suited to an imperial age of power politics, he had made
America's voice heard among the great powers. He had
been the model of the just man armed.

VI

"To Keep the
Left Center Together"

1905-1909

"I HAVE never known Congress to do quite as well as this Congress has done," the President wrote in August 1906, "and it seems to me that it is not often that an administration can say with greater truth than we can that we have carried out with signal success the policies we have undertaken." Still he was rather pessimistic on the party's prospects that November. For "judging from my experience of the past the time has about come for the swinging of the pendulum," he added, "and in such circumstances the people take the greatest satisfaction . . . in upsetting those who have done well."

The pendulum did not swing so far in 1906 as to defeat the Republicans nationally, yet Roosevelt accurately sensed the direction of American opinion. He had done much himself over the years to arouse this demand for reform. He had done something to satisfy it, too; and he would devote the remainder of his term to moving the G.O.P. toward the Left without straining party bonds to the breaking point. "To use the terminology of Continental politics," he would write in 1907, "I am trying to keep the left center together."

The Right had always regarded McKinley's successor with suspicion, but never more so than following the election of 1904. And after Roosevelt put through the bill to regulate railroad rates in 1906, the discontent within the Old Guard flared into open hostility. The President still managed the party organization capably enough to win the next nomination for his own candidate, William Howard Taft, but a deepening dispute with Congress precluded further reform legislation. Reduced to reliance upon the executive power alone, he fell into a snarling belligerency that boded ill for his party's future.

———

"I HAD no conception that there was such a tide in our favor," Roosevelt wrote after the great victory at the polls in November 1904, "and I frankly confess that I do not understand it." But he conceived that he had a vote of confidence in the Square Deal, and that as President by popular mandate he could take a bolder line in championing reform. His annual message to Congress in December sounded a new note of urgency in calling for federal legislation on corporations and labor. It signalled the beginning of a new phase in the struggle toward a just society.

The protective tariff was the key issue for many reformers, but they disagreed over how to lower it. Opposition of standpatters to any revision downward, moreover, was powerful. Roosevelt raised the question at once
and for a time considered incorporating some proposal
in his annual message. But fearing that he might endanger other parts of his legislative program that he deemed
more vital, he decided against a specific recommendation.
Anyway, revising tariff schedules was to him a matter of
expediency, not of principle. And he discerned that the
mere threat of tariff action could be a valuable weapon
in his fight for railroad regulation.

Railroad rates and rebates affected as broad a section
of the American public as the tariff. And though the
Old Guard opposed any further federal control of the
carriers, Roosevelt's study of the operation of the Elkins
Act had convinced him that it was "unwise and unsafe
from every standpoint to leave the question of rebates
where it now is, and to fail to give the Interstate Commerce Commission additional power of an effective kind
in regulating these rates." Armour, Standard Oil, and
other great corporations were abusing or circumventing
the anti-rebate law with impunity. The nation's ship-
pers and agrarians, chiefly in the South and West, were
up in arms over discriminatory rate practices. "On the interstate commerce business, which I regard as a matter
of principle," Roosevelt wrote, "I shall fight."

In his annual message the President came out strongly
for giving the ICC the power to set reasonable maximum
rates. He conceded that it was "undesirable, if it were

not impracticable, finally to clothe the commission with general authority to fix railroad rates." Yet the Supreme Court had ruled that under the Interstate Commerce Act of 1887 the commission did not even have the authority, upon finding a challenged rate unreasonable, to prescribe a maximum rate for the transportation in dispute. "In my judgment the most important legislative act now needed as regards the regulation of corporations is this act to confer on the Interstate Commerce Commission the power to revise rates and regulations," Roosevelt declared, "the revised rate to at once go into effect, and stay in effect unless and until the court of review reverses it."

A bill to implement this proposal progressed through the House so rapidly that it suggested that Speaker Cannon had consented to support it in return for the President's agreement to drop the tariff issue. Sent to the Senate by a vote of 326 to 17 in February 1905, the measure bogged down hopelessly in committee, however, as witness after witness testified against it on behalf of the railroads. Roosevelt accepted the delay philosophically, believing that by 1906 "we can get the issue so clearly drawn that the Senate will have to give in." Still he feared that "the big financiers" opposing further regulation would "force the moderates to join with the radicals in radical action, under penalty of not obtaining any at all." "I much prefer moderate action," he wrote, "but the ultraconservatives may make it necessary to accept what is radical."

Taking what he characteristically depicted as a middle-of-the-road position, Roosevelt maintained a constant pressure against the railroads' publicity campaign. And early the next year the House again passed a maximum-rate bill by an overwhelming majority. This new measure, sponsored by Representative Hepburn of Iowa, followed the prescription in the President's annual message of December 1905. It put under ICC supervision all private-car lines, refrigerator charges, and other devices used to circumvent the Elkins Act. It called for a uniform system of accounts, open to federal inspection, and for the expediting of legal cases involving the commerce statute. On the exact nature of the court review of ICC actions, the Hepburn bill was ambiguously silent, but subject to such appeal within thirty days, the commission would have the vital power, upon complaint and investigation, to fix a maximum rate.

In the Senate the standpatters led by Nelson Aldrich plotted Roosevelt's undoing. Aldrich engineered the report of the bill from committee unamended and without Republican endorsement. By arrangement with the minority leaders, he then had it committed on the floor to the charge of "Pitchfork Ben" Tillman of South Carolina, a demagogic Bryan Democrat who was not even on speaking terms with the President. Without party backing and hampered in leadership, the Roosevelt forces would find it most difficult to control the Senate. Amid the welter of amendments, the conservatives would hold out for a provision for judicial review of the facts as well as the procedure in any case decided by the commerce commission. If they were unable to defeat the bill outright, they hoped at least to weaken it by vesting super-vision of rate-fixing in the judiciary.

Embarrassed but not undone by Aldrich's tactics, Roo-sevelt adjusted his approach to his general objective. Working with Tillman through an intermediary, the President first moved toward the more radical propo-nents of regulation, seeking to fashion a coalition of "some fifteen or twenty Republicans added to most of the Democrats" behind an amendment restricting the railroads in any court review. When the Democratic cau-cus failed to agree upon such a restriction, Roosevelt shifted back toward the "ambiguous center" where he had started. His move antagonized the Left, but it at-tracted so much support among moderates that Aldrich had to retreat. Dropping their insistence upon broad court review, the conservative Republicans accepted a compromise that left the definition of the scope of re-view to the courts (really the Hepburn formula) but permitted injunctions to suspend ICC orders pending judicial decision. The battle for rate regulation was over.

Critics afterwards charged that Roosevelt had settled for too little. By obtaining court injunctions, the rail-roads would be able to delay the application of rate revi-sions. For lack of knowledge about the true worth of the roads, moreover, the commission would find it difficult to determine what a reasonable maximum rate should be. Robert M. La Follette contended that the President should have insisted upon physical evaluation of railroad properties as a basis for rate-making. The next year, in coming out for this very addition to the commerce law,

Roosevelt conceded the logic of the Wisconsin Senator's economic analysis.

But as Roosevelt had told La Follette in February 1906, "I want to get something through." Hence the President had refused to consider La Follette's physical evaluation scheme, which subsequently garnered only six Republican votes on a roll-call test. He had also opposed a Democratic amendment that would have deprived the courts of authority to issue injunctions suspending rate orders, because he and his aides thought that clearly unconstitutional. Roosevelt's attempt to work out some restriction acceptable to the more radical senators in both parties had been only a tactical maneuver; his preference all along had been for a moderate bill that would be constitutional yet effective. By going back to the Hepburn bill as it had passed the House, he had not forsaken principle or knuckled under to the conservatives. He had simply brought his party to support the limited reform he had advocated.

The Hepburn Act proved to be constitutional. In the first test of the scope of review, moreover, the courts rejected the broad interpretation favored by the ultraconservatives; the judiciary would only investigate the procedures, not the facts, in any ICC ruling. As the law gradually took effect, railroad men grew more bitter over Roosevelt's part in putting it through. And G.O.P. standpatters grew more rebellious, not just over rate legislation, but over mounting federal intervention generally.

The President aroused this concern in part by the pressure he built up for the Hepburn bill. In December 1905, for example, the federal government obtained grand jury indictments against the Chicago and Alton, the Great Northern, and several other western roads accused of secret rebating with packing companies. In March 1906, as the struggle over rates proceeded in the Senate, the President released a report of the Bureau of Corporations showing "that the Standard Oil Company has benefited enormously up almost to the present moment by secret rebates." At the same time he noted that an investigation of sugar shipments out of New York City indicated "that the sugar trust rarely, if ever, pays the lawful rate for transportation."

Beyond these revelations the Roosevelt administration in 1906 promoted other major reforms. For years the Department of Agriculture's chief chemist, Dr. Harvey Wiley, had been agitating for federal regulation of the labelling of foods and drugs, but his supporters had twice failed to get a House-approved pure-food measure past the Senate. In his annual message of 1905 Roosevelt finally recommended that "a law be enacted to regulate interstate commerce in misbranded and adulterated foods, drinks, and drugs." A muckraking exposure of the patent medicine industry in *Collier's* also helped to bring the Senate this time to a favorable vote. Then Upton Sinclair's attack in *The Jungle* upon the Chicago meat packers, together with personal appeals from the President, assisted the bill through the House. By making it illegal to manufacture or sell foods, drugs, medicines, or liquors which were adulterated or improperly labelled, the act carried federal intervention in private business a step further.

Sinclair's exposé sparked the more controversial effort in 1906 to extend federal supervision of meat packing. Fifteen years before, Congress had answered foreign complaints about diseased products from the United States by requiring ante mortem inspection of all cattle, sheep, and hogs whose meat was intended for export or interstate sale, and authorizing post mortem inspection at the discretion of the Secretary of Agriculture. But if *The Jungle* was to be believed, this regulation was a farce; through sharp practice and the most unsanitary conditions the great packers were continuing to endanger the public health. Though critical of the young author's socialist conclusions, Roosevelt promised Sinclair that "the specific evils you point out shall, if their existence be proved, and if I have the power, be eradicated."

Since the fairness of the Department's own probe of Sinclair's charges might be challenged, Roosevelt instructed Commissioner of Labor Neill and New York social worker James B. Reynolds to make an independent study of packing-house conditions. Their report substantially confirmed Sinclair's findings, but Roosevelt held back from publishing a document that could be so injurious to American livestock interests. Instead he warned that he would reveal the "hideous" details unless Congress took remedial action promptly. The Senate responded by approving the stiff regulations which Albert J. Beveridge, the reforming senator from Indiana, had drafted as an amendment to the agricultural appropriation bill.

But the "big stick" was less effective in the House,

where the agriculture committee framed a substitute that heeded most of the objections packers raised. His threat defied, the President transmitted the Neill-Reynolds report to Congress, but the committee gave ground grudgingly. It restored two major provisions it had deleted — to bar uninspected meat from interstate commerce and provide for the inspection (but not the dating) of canned meat and meat products — before reporting out the substitute. Then at the urging of Speaker Cannon, who feared a bitter division within the G.O.P., the committee also raised the annual appropriation for inspection from a barely adequate $1,000,000 to $3,000,-000, struck out the proviso that any company injured by a ruling could appeal "the legality or constitutionality of such ruling" in the federal courts, and made other concessions to tighter regulation. These changes still left the packers victorious over Beveridge on the dating of tins and the costs of inspection (Beveridge would have charged them a fee for each animal inspected), but Roosevelt, and eventually the Senate, accepted the compromise. On June 30, 1906, the President approved the regulations that thereafter governed meat inspection.

The large packers may actually have welcomed more effective inspection as a curb upon their smaller competitors. Yet the major producers clearly had opposed having "the management and control taken away from the men who have devoted their lives to the upbuilding and perfecting of this great American industry." As in the struggle over railroad rates, the most important issue had been control over private business, the most important question the breadth of court review. By leaving the role of the courts in a "purposeful ambiguity" interpreted later as requiring only a narrow procedural review, the meat-inspection amendment extended the scope of federal administrative rule. By granting authority to bar goods from interstate commerce to insure compliance, it enlarged the national police power.

In supporting this extension of federal authority Roosevelt adopted the same pragmatic approach he had on the Hepburn bill. He insisted that promises of good behavior from the meat packers were not enough, that it was "absolutely necessary" to have "legislation which will prevent the recurrence of these wrongs." As to the specific remedies, however, he was flexible. He did not at first think that Beveridge's requirement that the companies bear the cost of inspection was vital enough to "split or run the risk of losing the amendment," but after the House committee drafted its "ruinous" substitute, including only $1,000,000 annually for inspections, Roosevelt came out for the fee system. The $3,000,000 appropriation finally agreed upon was to him an adequate solution. Beveridge acknowledged that Congress would not have granted that, or anything else, "if Roosevelt had not picked up his big stick and smashed the packers . . . and their agents in the House and Senate."

The practical compromises the President pried out of Congress owed much to the radical agitation of writers like Upton Sinclair. But Roosevelt was not appreciative of their aid. Inevitably they demanded more reform and less expediency than a responsible political leader could afford. At the same time they were more critical of the conservative G.O.P., and of the capitalist system itself, than Roosevelt thought justified. Even as he moved left himself, he feared the drift toward class antagonism that might bring revolution. By carrying their attacks too far these journalists would only stiffen the resistance to needed intervention.

Disturbed most immediately by an acidulous attack upon high Republican officials by David Graham Phillips in a series on "The Treason of the Senate" for Hearst's *Cosmopolitan*, the President spoke out publicly against irresponsible journalism in April 1906 at the House Office Building dedication. Taking "the Man with the Muck-rake" in Bunyan's *Pilgrim's Progress* as his example, Roosevelt condemned "the man who never does anything else, who never thinks or speaks or writes, save of his feats with the muck-rake." He charged that by their "crude and sweeping generalizations" and "indiscriminate assault upon character" these sensationalists were misleading the public; they were failing to distinguish the good among the bad, and "if they gradually grow to feel that the whole world is nothing but muck, their power of usefulness is gone."

But "to denounce mudslinging," Roosevelt was most careful to point out, "does not mean the indorsement of whitewashing." He acknowledged that there was "filth on the floor, and it must be scraped up with a muck-rake." He did not intend to discourage "the most unsparing exposure of the politician who betrays his trust, of the big business man who makes or spends his fortune in illegitimate or corrupt ways." He just did not want to see the battle against evil turned indiscriminately into a struggle between "the haves" and "the have-nots." To vouch for his determination to fight for "lasting righteousness" he called for federal supervision over *all* corporations in interstate commerce, and congressional enactment of a progressive inheritance tax upon fortunes "swollen beyond all healthy limits."

The conservative press made much of Roosevelt's criticism of the newly-dubbed "muckrakers," but he had charted more radical objectives beyond the corporate regulations of 1906. He also took steps to improve the lot of laboringmen. He enforced the eight-hour law on government works more rigorously, and backed La Follette in putting through an employer's liability bill that applied to the District of Columbia and the common carriers. In addition, the President asked that Congress provide for government investigation of strikes involving interstate commerce, and federal regulation of the procedure by which courts issued injunctions. But Congress did not even approve (until 1907) his recommendation that the Bureau of Labor be empowered to investigate the condition of labor of women and children. "I do not think that Congress was quite wise in their treatment of the labor people," he wrote as the election of 1906 approached. "It is a bad business to solidify labor against us."

Roosevelt had cause for worry. The AF of L leaders, outraged especially at a sweeping court order against their boycott of a St. Louis stove company, had launched an aggressive campaign in 1906 to defeat Speaker Cannon and other Old Guardsmen who had opposed anti-injunction legislation. At the same time the Socialists, who had increased their vote from 100,000 in 1900 to 400,000 in 1904, were exerting a more powerful influence upon muckrakers and middle-class reformers. William Jennings Bryan opened the canvass for the Democrats that fall in Madison Square Garden with a host of radical proposals, including government ownership of railways and abolition of injunctions in all labor cases. Bryan "came a bad cropper" among Eastern editors with his "preposterous positions," Roosevelt noted, but "he is by no means as dead as the New York Democratic and independent papers . . . wish to persuade themselves is the case."

Defending the moderate reforms put through Congress in 1906, Roosevelt valiantly tried to straddle the widening differences within his own party. From the standpatter Cannon to the increasingly radical Beveridge, he supported G.O.P. candidates. In his one major speech at Harrisburg, he denounced "reactionaries" on the one hand and "foolish extremists" on the other. But the more conservative Republicans thought that he was leaning too far left, particularly when at Harrisburg he discovered an "inherent power" beyond the enumerated powers in the Constitution for "a constantly increasing supervision over and control of the great fortunes used in business." Railway king E. H. Harriman refused to contribute to the party because of the administration's actions. So did Standard Oil officials and many Wall Street financiers. "We have suffered very much," Roosevelt noted on election eve, "from lack of funds."

Apart from Kansas and Iowa, the Republicans held their own at the polls in 1906 against organized labor and the Democracy. But while Roosevelt interpreted the result as an endorsement of his policies, ultraconservatives took heart at the resounding victories of Cannon in Illinois and Foraker in Ohio, as well as the marked decline in the Socialist tally. The forces to the left had suffered a defeat, but those to the right and in the center differed widely on its cause. That disagreement threatened trouble for a President who intended to press the Old Guard still further in the direction of reform. "I do wish," Roosevelt remarked of the protests at his renewed call for more federal regulation in December 1906, "that the same men who get elected on the issue of standing by me would not at once turn and try to thwart me."

His annual message to Congress that December reiterated his demands for a progressive inheritance tax and federal supervision of all companies engaged in interstate commerce. He again asserted the government's interest in corporate relations with labor by calling for "compulsory investigation" of major disputes. The President then proposed that the Interstate Commerce Commission be authorized to use the physical evaluation of rail properties as a basis to fix rates — the very scheme that La Follette had advanced during the Hepburn bill debates. "La Follette often does real good in the Senate," Roosevelt remarked in January 1907, "and I like him a great deal better this year than last."

But Roosevelt faced a mounting attack from the embattled conservatives. In these last two years of his term, with his power of patronage much reduced, they were bolder in their opposition, exploiting extraneous issues (such as his "simplified spelling" reform) and charging that his assaults upon big business, by undermining public confidence, had produced the stock market decline in 1907. By the time the panic struck Wall Street in October, they would have the President on the defensive.

His spelling reform had roots in that same pride in country that made Roosevelt such a nationalist about everything from foreign policy to aesthetic taste. Only months after taking office, he had initiated an extensive "restoration" of the White House, selecting McKim, Mead and White, a leading architectural firm, to transform it "from a shabby likeness to the ground floor of the Astor House into a simple and dignified dwelling for the head of a great republic." American coinage was "artistically of atrocious hideousness" as well; at the President's suggestion the Treasury employed Augustus Saint-Gaudens, the sculptor, to design the ten- and twenty-dollar gold pieces finally minted in 1907. "I do not wish there to be the slightest interference with Saint-Gaudens in connection with the coinage from its artistic side," Roosevelt declared, but he changed the master's plan of the ten-dollar coin himself by replacing a wreath with an Indian feather bonnet.

No traditionalist about the English language, Roosevelt thought the simplified "American" forms advocated by the anti-colonialist Spelling Reform Association would "make our spelling a little less foolish and fan-tastic." He therefore directed the government printer in August 1906 to use the new style (involving three hundred changes such as "thru" for "through," "honor" for "honour," and "mist" for "missed") in publications of the executive department. The Supreme Court disre-garded the recommendation, however, and the House of Representatives passed a resolution forbidding any departures from standard spelling in publications author-ized by law. With his conservative opponents already complaining about "executive usurpation," Roosevelt quickly confined the reform to his own correspond-ence.

A more serious controversy arose out of his discharge of three Negro army companies implicated in a shooting affray at Brownsville, Texas. None of these soldiers ad-mitted to knowing who had stormed through that town one night in August 1906 firing shots that killed one citi-zen, but white witnesses and circumstantial evidence convinced army investigators that some of the Negroes must have participated; the others were just shielding them by "a conspiracy of silence." Since the "men ap-pear to stand together in a determination to resist the detection of guilt," the Inspector-General of the Army concluded, "they should stand together when the pen-alty falls." Immediately before the November election the President ordered the 160 men "discharged without honor" (six of them held the Medal of Honor) and "for-ever barred from re-enlistment."

Roosevelt at first refused to heed the many protests

through the North at this stern verdict. And when Foraker of Ohio took up the soldiers' cause in the Senate, the President conjectured that this conservative "has been representing Wall Street in attacking me on this issue." The audacious Ohioan did have a relationship with Standard Oil that would eventually retire him from public life in disgrace, but he presented enough evidence of the troops' innocence to convince the Senate in January 1907 of the need for an investigation of the Brownsville case. He persisted so ably in his defense, moreover, that the President in 1909 accepted a compromise measure setting up a special military court to hear those denying any implication in the incident. Of the eighty-four soldiers who testified before this tribunal, fourteen were finally declared eligible for reinstatement.

This judgment could not atone for an edict that Roosevelt was reluctant to admit had been too harsh. Nor could it silence accusations that he had discriminated against Negroes — a charge that he denied and tried to counter by championing the colored man's equal rights as a citizen. And it could not have any effect upon the use to which conservatives had put the Brownsville affair. For as Foraker had developed his evidence, they had found support for their contention that the Chief Executive was impetuous and irresponsible.

Under heavy attack for his imperious attitude, Roosevelt in 1907 began to suffer still heavier criticism for the stock market's decline. The first break on Wall Street came in January, after John D. Rockefeller warned publicly that the President's interference with big business would harm the country's prosperity. The market rallied only to fall more sharply in March, upon rumors that the federal government intended some dramatic new move against the railroad empire of E. H. Harriman. "I would hate to tell you," Harriman remarked after Union Pacific fell twenty-five points in a day, "to whom I think you ought to go for an explanation of all this."

Harriman had been feuding with Roosevelt ever since railroad rates became an issue in 1904. A prominent contributor to the G.O.P. that year, Harriman thought that he should have been consulted upon ICC recommendations, but Roosevelt denied that in requesting the magnate's aid in the campaign he had encouraged that belief. The breach between the two men became irreparable after the New York *World* purchased and printed a purloined Harriman letter that provoked the President in April 1907 to publish his own account of their dealings in 1904. The "real trouble" with the "Harriman-Standard Oil combination and the other owners of predatory wealth," Roosevelt privately concluded, was that they had "never before been obliged really to reckon with the federal government."

Roosevelt rejected the blame for falling prices in rail securities. He also refused to back down on his request that the ICC recommend legislation on the physical valuation of railroad property, the supervision of rail stock and bond issues, and "some system of national incorporation or national license which would give the national government far-reaching control over all railroads engaged in interstate commerce." As the Department of Justice in July 1907 filed suit under the Sherman Act to dissolve the American Tobacco Company and readied a similar action against Harriman's Union Pacific-Southern Pacific lines, Roosevelt prepared to strike back at his critics by advocating criminal prosecutions of big businessmen who violated the federal antitrust law.

Before the President delivered this new attack, District Judge Kenesaw M. Landis handed down a fine of over $25,000,000 on Standard Oil on 1,462 counts of rebating, and another severe drop in stock prices brought a fresh rain of protests down upon Oyster Bay. Insisting that he was not appreciably responsible for a monetary crisis that was really worldwide, Roosevelt still went to Provincetown in August to denounce "certain malefactors of great wealth" who were encouraging panic in hope of reversing the administration's policies. But he betrayed his uneasiness by encouraging the Attorney General to be more cautious in trust prosecutions; by September, Roosevelt was relieved that "my Provincetown speech did not ruin matters, for they have improved steadily since."

Credit remained so tight on Wall Street, however, that any faltering in confidence could start a dangerous reaction. And when the collapse of a spectacular copper speculation forced the Knickerbocker Trust Company to close its doors in October 1907, panic threatened the city's other financial institutions. The Secretary of the Treasury quickly deposited $25,000,000 in government funds in New York national banks, but emergency measures could not keep stocks from slumping disastrously as currency disappeared and call rates on loans rose. The situation remained critical for several trust companies; indeed, by the first week in November it was rumored that when the exchange opened on Monday the investment house of Moore and Schley might go down. If that happened, the Trust Company of North America might also close, and the whole credit structure topple.

At this juncture two United States Steel executives sped to Washington with a proposal to stave off that danger. Interrupting the President's breakfast on Monday, November 4, Judge Elbert H. Gary and Henry C. Frick explained to Roosevelt and Root that "a certain business firm" would "undoubtedly fail this week" unless it received help. To save this company, which held a majority of the securities of Tennessee Coal and Iron but could not dispose of them in the tight market, U. S. Steel was willing to purchase that stock at a "price somewhat in excess of . . . its real value." But since that purchase would be criticized as monopolistic, even though their company still would not control over sixty per cent of the country's steel properties, Gary and Frick said "they did not wish to do this if I stated that it ought not to be done." The President replied that "while of course I could not advise them to take the action proposed, I felt it no public duty of mine to interpose any objection."

For $45,000,000 U. S. Steel thereupon acquired a company with mineral resources worth far more than that, but Moore and Schley did not fall. Moreover, by this and other action it took in November to alleviate the currency stringency, the administration did much to turn the economy toward recovery. By December the worst of the crisis was over.

Far from being chastened, Roosevelt was angrier than ever at conservatives who blamed him for the panic. He would be just as angry at the charge, raised in the campaigns of 1908 and 1912, that his assent to the Tennessee Coal and Iron purchase had been unwarranted. The fact was that Moore and Schley might have been saved in some other fashion, but Roosevelt could not have known that. He had had to act quickly, and if he trusted Gary's word unduly, it was because U. S. Steel had been so cooperative in revealing its affairs to the Bureau of Corporations. In fact, the informal understanding which federal officials had developed with the steel executives was almost the prototype of the formal supervision that Roosevelt wanted Congress to adopt over all interstate corporations.

Never an opponent of combinations for their size alone, the President had created the Bureau of Corporations in 1903 on the theory that the "mere letting in of light" would remedy many of the objectionable practices by which they attained and maintained their positions. But to obtain the necessary information was difficult, Bureau chief James R. Garfield found, unless corporations volunteered it, and this they were unlikely to do if it would be used against them in court. In May 1904 Garfield and the Attorney General agreed to an International Harvester proposal that if the company conformed to the anti-rebating law after being informed of violations, there would be no prosecution. In November 1905, at a White House conference with Garfield and Roosevelt, Judge Gary consented to open the steel company books with the understanding that any disagreement on the use of the material would be decided ultimately by the President.

Gary's cooperative approach made U. S. Steel appear to be a "good" trust to Roosevelt, but other corporations did not fare so well. The meat packers, for example, had provided Garfield with information that he thought should be privileged, but in January 1905, reversing an earlier ruling, the President directed the Bureau to work with the Justice Department in proceedings against the beef trust. Standard Oil officials were even more amenable to some arrangement with Garfield, but it was never consummated, and Roosevelt publicized the Bureau's findings on Standard to good effect in putting through the Hepburn bill. To him, as to so many Americans, the great oil refiner could only be a "bad" trust.

Roosevelt failed to see the dangers in an administration that could thus discriminate among private companies. But he did see that the federal government was carrying on dual operations that came into conflict. The Bureau and the Justice Department frequently disagreed on the use of the information they had gathered. More than that, Garfield was developing through the informal understandings an alternative system of control that clashed with the Attorney General's prosecutions. Of the two methods of corporate regulation, Roosevelt increasingly preferred the flexible managerial approach of the Bureau to "the sweeping and indiscriminate prohibition of all combinations which has been so marked and as I think so mischievous a feature of our anti-trust legislation." In the same way he favored pooling agreements among railroads — so long as the ICC had adequate supervisory power.

Responsive to the President's call in December 1907 for the extension of federal supervision over all interstate corporations, Representative Hepburn introduced the National Civic Federation's bill to formalize the detente that Garfield had worked out with U. S. Steel. But though Roosevelt was "mighty glad" about the Federation's action, and even sent up a special message in its support, the coalition behind it was too fragile, the opposition too widespread. Business advocates like Foraker thought the Sherman Act should be amended to permit "reasonable" restraints of trade, but without requiring a company to register vital data with the Bureau in order to enjoy this benefit. Antitrust spokesmen like La Follette approved of fuller reports to the government, but without any weakening of the Sherman Act. And labor leaders like Gompers only backed the bill because it also removed unions and strikes from the jurisdiction of the antitrust statute; if this provision was altered, as seemed likely in view of businessmen's objections, then the measure was surely doomed.

The President had his own reservations about legalizing the blacklist and the boycott, but his main worry was that Congress might follow Foraker and turn over anti-

trust action to "the chaos and inefficiency necessarily produced by an effort to use the courts as the prime instru-
ment for administering such a law." Roosevelt wanted
"the full power given to the *Executive* officers in the matter of the Sherman Antitrust Law." Rather than have
control pass to the judiciary, he would have no change at
all. "I do not think the present law is wise," he wrote in
March 1908, "but I think it would be much more unwise to amend it by leaving the matter to be fought out
after the event before the courts, or by giving the courts
any original power in the matter."

Roosevelt's determination blocked reactionary plans
to weaken the Sherman Act. His concern for preserving
executive power also distinguished him from leading
eastern supporters of the Hepburn bill like George W.
Perkins, whose principal aim was to protect big business
from meddlesome interference by the states. Yet in his
regulatory program the President was closer to Perkins
than to midwesterners in the agrarian tradition like La
Follette, who wanted to break up combinations through
rigorous enforcement of the Sherman Law. By 1908 the
differences over antitrust policy that divided the left
center of the party were clearly emerging along sectional
lines. By settling for a continuation of the dual operations of the Bureau and the Department of Justice, Roosevelt for the moment composed a serious disagreement
within reform ranks.

This effort to extend federal supervision of corporations was part of a general enlargement of government
intervention that Roosevelt advocated after the panic

of 1907. The great majority of the proposals he advanced suffered the same fate. Congress did not empower the ICC to determine railway valuations or to regulate rail securities. Nor did it act on an inheritance and income tax, the limitation of labor injunctions, compulsory investigation of large labor disputes, and extension of the eight-hour law. About all it did for Roosevelt's "campaign against privilege" was to revise a 1906 employer's liability act for interstate carriers to meet the Supreme Court's objections, and pass a "model" child labor law affecting only the District of Columbia and the territories. In fact, the one major piece of domestic legislation was a currency measure supported by conservative eastern financiers and strenuously opposed by La Follette and other insurgent Republicans west of the Mississippi.

This dismal record reflected the hostility that had developed between the Chief Executive and the more conservative elements in the G.O.P. Their mutual criticism had reached new heights after the October panic. Roosevelt's annual message to Congress in December showed his bitterness, but the next month, after the Supreme Court declared the earlier employer's liability act unconstitutional, he sent up a blistering special message. Repeating all his demands for more authority to protect laboringmen and control corporations, the President further recommended measures "to prevent at least the grosser forms of gambling in securities and commodities."

He then launched a spirited defense of his administration against the attacks inspired by "certain wealthy men" who had "banded together to work for a reaction." Through their "puppets" in public life, the press, and the colleges, Roosevelt charged, they were seeking "to overthrow and discredit all who honestly administer the law . . . and to secure if possible a freedom from all restraint which will permit every unscrupulous wrongdoer to do what he wishes unchecked provided he has enough money." In particular he condemned the Standard Oil Trust and "certain notorious railroad combinations," as well as judges who made "the wageworker feel with bitterness that the courts are hostile to him." This blazing indictment spared no opponent of "the moral regeneration of the business world."

Had Roosevelt yielded to the temptation to fight for these convictions by running for the Presidency himself in 1908, the party behind him would have been seriously divided. For in trying "to keep the left center together" he had so alienated the conservatives that only the thought that Roosevelt would soon be gone kept them halfway loyal. Appearing to Roosevelt "as blind to some of the tendencies of the time, as the French noblesse was before the French Revolution," they were even reluctant to support William Howard Taft as his chosen successor. They would go along with that nomination simply because they could do no other, and because in office the legal-minded Taft might prove more amenable to their views.

The compulsions of politics made it easier to avoid an open break. Indeed, as the Republican convention approached, Roosevelt backed away from extremism to reaffirm his stand within the center of the party. He told Lodge he wanted "a straight, thoro-going platform as free from the Hale type of reactionary policy as from the La Follette type of fool radicalism." He accepted a plank on the limitation of injunctions that was to the right of that prescription. And though he would have preferred a reformer like Beveridge for the vice-presidential candidate, he finally settled for the Old Guard's choice of James S. Sherman of New York. Confident that Taft "will carry on the work substantially as I have carried it on," Roosevelt put party harmony above policy differences to win the election of 1908.

But by words no less than deeds, the outgoing President had excited hopes that Taft would find it difficult to satisfy. Roosevelt had achieved as much as he had in federal legislation through a wise choice of objectives and a skillful application of power. He had avoided the most troublesome domestic issue in postponing tariff revision; yet he had aroused such opposition among congressional leaders that after 1906 his legislative efforts had been fruitless. Smarting under conservative criticism, Roosevelt had defiantly delivered the most radical message of his career. He had espoused a reform program that rallied adherents to "the progressive principles of the party." As he prepared to turn over command, the struggle for control within the G.O.P. had clearly been joined.

VII

"We Stand at Armageddon and We Battle for the Lord"

1909-1912

"I VERY EMPHATICALLY FEEL that to me personally to be nominated in 1912 would be a calamity," Roosevelt wrote Judge Ben Lindsey in December 1911.

Ever since returning from his African expedition the year before, he had been resisting suggestions from Lindsey and other reformers that he make himself available for the presidential nomination in 1912. Though ever more antagonistic toward his successor, Roosevelt had persistently refused to support any insurgent move to supplant Taft as G.O.P. standard bearer.

Yet he had refused also to put himself definitely out of the running, for "circumstances might conceivably arise when I should feel that there was a duty to the people which I could not shirk."

The party crisis was rooted in the same conflict that had marred Roosevelt's last years in the White House. But Roosevelt had sided with the reformers, whereas Taft had since leaned toward the conservatives. Antagonized especially by the new President's inept handling of tariff and conservation issues, Republican insurgents had formed a more cohesive faction dedicated to "the progressive principles of the party." They had turned for leadership to the man most prominently identified with those principles. Much as he desired to preserve harmony, Roosevelt had been drawn toward a fateful struggle with his once esteemed friend.

Troubled and uncertain, Theodore Roosevelt knew in December 1911 that he had reached another parting of the ways. This time — unlike 1884 — morality would triumph over expediency. In barely two months' time, calamity or no, he would take the road that led to Armageddon.

THE CLASH in 1912 would be particularly bitter because he was most responsible for the choice of his successor. Having taken himself out of contention for 1908 in a statement which opponents later charged applied to 1912 as well, Roosevelt surveyed possible candidates carefully. He preferred Elihu Root for experience and executive skill, but the Secretary of State's reputation as a big businessman's advocate made nomination and election too unlikely. So the selection narrowed to Secretary of War William Howard Taft of Ohio, or another lawyer, Charles Evans Hughes, reform governor of New York since 1905.

"Hughes has been a good Governor," Roosevelt admitted privately in July 1907; "I think he would make a good President." But Hughes did "not begin to compare with Taft, either morally, intellectually, or in knowledge of public problems." Reactionary elements "would all prefer Hughes because they would hope that his unfamiliarity with the needs of the country as a whole, and his lawyer-like conservatism, would make him a President like Cleveland instead of a President like me." And then Hughes was too independent, too determined to get on in politics "without being under obligations to anyone." He was simply not Roosevelt's man.

Taft, on the other hand, was a personal friend and political associate of long standing. He was a capable administrator with extraordinary experience in military and foreign affairs. Had he desired it, he could have had an Associate Judgeship on the Supreme Court in 1906, but Taft, prodded by his wife, rejected that in hope of gaining the greater prize two years later. From the spring of 1907 on, Roosevelt did all he could — short of a public pronouncement — to see that Taft prevailed on the first ballot.

The reluctance that many exhibited at accepting his choice only made Roosevelt the more insistent. Reactionaries opposed Taft because they wanted "a reversal of the policies for which Taft and I stand"; if they prevailed, he wrote, "you can say good-bye to tariff reform." Many reformers opposed Taft, on the other hand, because they preferred Roosevelt; indeed, "nothing could have prevented my renomination," he asserted in May

1908, "excepting the most resolute effort on my part to get someone else accepted as representing me and nominated in my place." In Roosevelt's mind, at least, Taft was sure "to carry on the work upon which we have entered during the past six years."

Roosevelt manifested no misgivings about "lawyer-like conservatism" on his friend's part. Nor did he seem concerned about the difficulties Taft would face in guiding a divided party. But perhaps in part because he recalled how he had felt in taking over from McKinley, Roosevelt began to lay plans for an extended African expedition upon leaving office. A great hunt would be high adventure; it would also gather valuable specimens for American museums. But "I know you felt as I did," he informed the journey's patron, Andrew Carnegie, in July 1909, "that for a year or so it was a good thing for me to be out of the United States."

Nominated and elected as his mentor had planned, William Howard Taft was properly grateful. Yet he sensed the troublous times ahead. In taking up tariff reform he would have to work closely with Speaker Cannon and Senator Aldrich, even as Roosevelt had, but the midwestern insurgents would be alarmed at those tactics. Without Roosevelt's skill at handling the press, Taft feared that soon "a large part of the public will feel as if I had fallen away from your ideals; but you know me better and will understand that I am still working away on the same old plan." Came the departing hunter's reply: "Everything will surely turn out all right, old man."

Roosevelt sincerely hoped that things would turn out all right. And though he thought it unwise to attack the tariff issue so aggressively, he recognized Taft's need to assert himself independently. There were bound to be "worries and bothers" over a new tariff bill, he assured Root and Lodge, for "what we have to meet is not an actual need, but a mental condition among our people, who believe there ought to be a change."

But the tariff debate had more than a fleeting importance. When Aldrich reported an amended bill revising rates upward, a group of midwestern Republican insurgents who called themselves "progressives" took the Senate floor to criticize the intricate changes. Led by La Follette of Wisconsin and Dolliver of Iowa, this small yet vocal band identified themselves with the Roosevelt tradition; they attacked their regular opponents as subservient to trusts, and called upon the President for aid in fulfilling his campaign promises.

A low-tariff man since his student days at Yale under William Graham Sumner, Taft attempted to assist in the fight. But he lacked Roosevelt's skill at legislative maneuver, and the concessions he obtained from Aldrich and Cannon did not satisfy the progressive Republicans. More unfortunately, Taft gradually concluded he had "really a good bill" that represented "a revision substantially downward." On a speaking tour that fall, in a hastily prepared address at Winona, Minnesota, he boldly defended the regulars who had supported "on the whole . . . the best [tariff] bill that the Republican party ever passed."

That statement obscured his reasoned defense and irritated a public already pinched by rising living costs.
It also exacerbated his relations with the insurgents who
had voted against the Payne-Aldrich bill; after Winona
they openly criticized him for lining up with the eastern
conservatives. The *Des Moines Register and Leader*
was not the only Republican paper to declare that the
1912 nomination was Roosevelt's for the asking.

The cry against "Aldrichism" would not have sustained the incipient "back from Elba" movement among
Roosevelt admirers after Winona. But in the autumn of
1909 further controversy arose over the administration's
policy on conservation. Here was an area to which Roosevelt had been particularly devoted, and where his bold
actions had won the praise of progressive-minded citizens. If Taft fell away from the Roosevelt example, he
would be in real trouble politically.

Through seven years as President, Roosevelt had
championed the cause of conservation. He had successfully supported the Newlands irrigation and reclamation
bill over Cannon's opposition. He had also obtained a
measure broadening the power of a more efficient United
States Forest Service within the Department of Agriculture. He had backed Chief Forester Gifford Pinchot
in adding forty-three million acres to the National For-
ests, and withdrawing over twenty-five hundred potential water-power sites and sixty-three million acres of
coal lands from entry pending controlled development
through regulated leasing. Roosevelt had created five
National Parks, proclaimed sixteen National Monuments,

and established fifty-one wildlife refuges. Through an Inland Waterways Commission and a Governors' Conference he had inspired intelligent planning for the future.

By these deeds he had inspired vociferous criticism as well. Western interests had been particularly exercised at the way in which he and Pinchot had treated an amendment to the Agricultural Appropriation bill in 1907 specifying that no forest reserve should thereafter be created within six northwestern states "except by act of Congress." Had he signed that measure at once, the President would have lost executive power over millions of acres of public lands which the Forest Service had long considered suitable for the National Reserves. When the bill reached his desk, however, he had authorized Pinchot to prepare final papers keeping those lands safely in federal custody. On March 2, 1907, before expiration of the ten days he had to consider the appropriation bill, Roosevelt had formally proclaimed twenty-three new reserves totalling sixteen million acres in the six states affected.

"If Congress differs from me . . . it will have full opportunity in the future to take such positions as it may desire anent the discontinuance of the reserves," Roosevelt had written in defense of his "midnight" proclamations, but protests of aggrieved congressmen had come to nothing. And for every conservative critic of his executive methods there had been a radical supporter who lauded the principles he applied to the public domain. Conservation policy touched so many different interests, large and small, federal and state, that few actions were without ambiguous effects. But in so far as he had power, express or implied, Roosevelt as President had impressed the nation with the importance of its great resources for future generations.

Pinchot had stayed on as Chief Forester under the new administration, but James R. Garfield had been replaced as Secretary of the Interior by Richard A. Ballinger of Seattle, formerly (1907-08) Commissioner of the Land Office. A westerner and an individualist, Ballinger had indicated as Commissioner that he preferred outright sale to the "socialist" mineral-lease policies of Garfield and Pinchot. A lawyer of the strict-construction school, he had soon indicated as Secretary that he thought Garfield had acted without proper authority in protecting possible water-power sites by withdrawing public lands from entry. Ballinger's views had suited Taft's basic aim to put the reform demand aroused by Roosevelt "into legal execution." "Pinchot is not a lawyer," Taft had written in June 1909, "and I am afraid he is quite willing to camp outside the law to accomplish his beneficent purposes."

On evidence gathered by an Interior Department official, L. R. Glavis, Pinchot had shortly concluded that Ballinger himself had been illegally assisting some Seattle businessmen to turn over Alaskan coal lands to the Morgan-Guggenheim syndicate. When Taft exonerated the Secretary and authorized Glavis's dismissal, Pinchot had continued to feed anti-Ballinger material to Glavis and the press. In November 1909 Glavis exposed the whole controversy in *Collier's Weekly*, in December insurgent congressmen demanded an investigation, in January Pinchot criticized the President in a letter that Dolliver read to the Senate. Reluctantly, knowing how Roosevelt would react, Taft finally dismissed the Chief Forester.

Pinchot deserved the dismissal he had courted, but from a political standpoint Taft should have obtained Ballinger's resignation as well. For though a congressional investigation eventually cleared the Secretary of charges of corruption, it amply demonstrated that he was no true friend of conservation. It revealed also that the lengthy legal analysis on which Taft had supposedly based his opinion clearing Ballinger had been predated by three months, a not unusual practice in government, but a grave error where official honesty was in question. At the bar of public opinion, Taft and Ballinger came away the losers.

Ballinger was to resign in March 1911, to be replaced by a friend of Pinchot's whose devotion to conservation was unchallenged. But the President's stubborn loyalty to Ballinger meantime did great political damage. Rallying to Pinchot's cause, the insurgents gained enough strength in Congress to curb Speaker Cannon's powers and disrupt the conservative Republican program. And Pinchot's removal put a heavy strain upon Taft's tie with Roosevelt. Almost unconsciously, Taft prepared himself for a break by finding fault privately with Roosevelt's cavalier treatment of the law on public lands. On his part, Roosevelt became more suspicious of his successor's dedication to the ideals they had seemed to share.

Taft's failure to reappoint Garfield had long irritated Roosevelt; the first news of Pinchot's dismissal made him "most uneasy" in far-off Africa. "I cannot think of a man in the country whose loss would be a more real misfortune to the Nation than yours would be," he had told the Chief Forester in March 1909; a year later came confirmation of the loss in a Pinchot letter indicting Taft's policies. "It is a very ungracious thing for an ex-President to criticize his successor," Roosevelt replied, "and yet I cannot as an honest man cease to battle for the principles for which you and I and Jim [Garfield] and Moody and the rest of our close associates stood." At once he planned to see Pinchot before returning home, "before I in even the smallest degree commit myself."

In Italy in April 1910 Gifford Pinchot laid before the returning naturalist the full bill of particulars, documented by letters from men like Dolliver, Beveridge, and William Allen White. Roosevelt, however anxious to give Taft "the benefit of every doubt," concluded that the President and Congress had "on many important points completely twisted around the policies I advocated and acted upon." "I don't think that under the Taft-Aldrich-Cannon régime there has been a real appreciation of the needs of the country," he informed Lodge, "and I am certain that there has been no real appreciation of the way the country felt." In a clear slap at Taft's basic approach, he contended that "an Administration which is primarily a lawyers' Administration" was "totally unfit" to give the "aggressive leadership" demanded by the people.

Apprised that many insurgents were already talking "Roosevelt against Taft" for 1912, he expressed to Lodge "the very strongest objection" to having to run in what could well be a hopeless cause, "staggering under a load . . . put on my shoulders through no fault of my own." Nor did he see how he could take part in the upcoming congressional elections. He would not "be put into the attitude of antagonizing my friends, or criticizing my successor"; he would also not "be put into the attitude of failing to stand for the great principles which I regard as essential." Under the circumstances, silence seemed the part of wisdom.

A conference with Elihu Root in London in late May stiffened Roosevelt's resolve to keep "out of things political." A "most poignant" letter of accounting from Taft, to be followed later in June 1910 by an hour's conference at the President's summer place in Massachusetts, strengthened Roosevelt's hope that the administration might yet be saved. "Taft has passed his nadir," Roosevelt argued to Pinchot in late June, and "independently of outside pressure he will try to act with greater firmness, and to look at things more from . . . the interests of the people, and less from the standpoint of a technical lawyer." That being so, Taft "may and probably will turn out a perfectly respectable President . . . who . . . will have done well enough to justify us in renominating him."

Foreseeing "very ugly times" for himself if Taft were not renominated in 1912, Roosevelt channeled his energy into finding "a common ground upon which Insurgents and Regulars can stand." Refusing to take sides in any senatorial primaries, he maintained that Republican differences were not over principle. Refusing to accept the term "progressive" in a factional sense, he sought to develop a "progressive" program to which the bulk of the G.O.P. could subscribe. "The safest thing to me," he counseled, "seems to be to dwell as far as possible on the future."

It was in this spirit of rallying a disunited party that Roosevelt carefully planned a major address for August 31, 1910, in dedicating the John Brown battlefield at Osawatomie, Kansas. Into that speech went many of his proposals to Congress in 1907 and 1908 — government supervision of all interstate corporations, physical valuation of railroads, graduated taxes on income and inheritances, revision of the nation's financial system, conservation of natural resources, workmen's compensation, regulation of the terms and conditions of labor. In addition he espoused tariff revision by an expert commission, the direct primary, and a corrupt practices act. He cast all this into a broad argument for a powerful central government that placed human rights before property rights, the national need before sectional or personal advantage.

This "New Nationalism" paralleled rather than reflected the views in Herbert Croly's *The Promise of American Life* (1909), a copy of which Roosevelt had obtained in London in June. Roosevelt had developed his own rationale of "Hamiltonian means for Jeffersonian ends" over many years, but he did adopt some of Croly's terminology (such as "the New Nationalism").

Croly's criticism of the neutral implications of the "Square Deal" may also have sharpened the definition at Osawatomie. "When I say that I am for the square deal, I mean not merely that I stand for fair play under the present rules of the game," Roosevelt asserted, "but that I stand for having those rules changed so as to work for a more substantial equality of opportunity and of reward for equally good service." As ever excepting the poor man who refused to try to help himself, Roosevelt forthrightly advocated a positive role for the national government in promoting a more just and democratic society.

As an effort at a "progressive" compromise between insurgents and regulars, however, the Osawatomie manifesto failed. For much as it warned against unjustified interference with property rights, it seemed to conservatives to place Roosevelt among the John Browns, not the Abraham Lincolns. They castigated him for quoting Lincoln to the effect that "Labor is prior to, and independent of capital. . . . Labor is the superior of capital." They indicted him for again attacking the judiciary for establishing a "neutral ground" where "lawbreakers of great wealth" could find refuge (as in the Knight and Lochner cases) from either state or national power. Though he later took a more moderate line in the East, they continued to accuse him of "Over-Radicalism."

Insurgents, on the other hand, welcomed his views. Ever since Taft and the regular leaders in March had decided to campaign against "progressives" in the primaries, a bitter party struggle had been in progress. In state after state, "Taft Republican" clubs had sprung up to battle "Progressive Republicans." The Republican National Committee had supplied funds and speakers, the President had wielded the patronage power to purge those legislators who had opposed the administration's policies. The rebels had fired back so tellingly that beginning in Indiana and Iowa during June they had inflicted severe defeats upon the standpat faction. They looked to Roosevelt's western swing to help carry Michigan, Wisconsin, and Washington in September 1910.

Taft meantime had continued to hope that his old mentor might still endorse the administration. But after Osawatomie the President forsook any thought of a reconciliation. Long convinced that the insurgents really aimed to push him aside in 1912, Taft became equally sure that Roosevelt had his mind set on running then himself. Taft also admitted finally to being a conservative, opposed to socialistic reforms and assaults upon court decisions. "The thing of all others that I am not going to do," he wrote his brother, "is to step out of the way of Mr. Roosevelt when he is advocating such wild ideas as those . . . in the Osawatomie speech."

Eventually, to the insurgents' dismay, Roosevelt did go so far as to praise Taft's achievements (but not to back him for 1912) before the New York state convention that endorsed the Payne-Aldrich tariff and nominated a Taft man for 1912, Henry L. Stimson, for governor. But expediency could not carry New York or most other eastern states in 1910. Only in those western areas where progressivism had taken strongest hold —

Wisconsin, Iowa, Kansas, Nebraska, the Dakotas, Minnesota, California, Washington — did the Republican party emerge relatively unscathed. "We have had a smashing defeat," Roosevelt confessed to a British friend, but then "the situation was really impossible." Indeed, "the best thing that could happen to us now would be to do what we can with Taft, face probable defeat in 1912, and then endeavor to reorganize under really capable and sanely progressive leadership."

Had Roosevelt held to that political strategy he could have avoided personal disaster in 1912 and possibly won nomination and election in 1916. Certainly he tried for many months to pursue that very course. But the party division that had drawn him into the 1910 campaign only grew more decided, until some contest against Taft's candidacy was inevitable. At the same time the President's actions at home and abroad further alienated his former chief. Beguiled by ambition for power and by a sense of duty to the "plain people," Roosevelt at last came to believe the demand for him might just be strong enough to win the party's nomination in 1912. Forsaking his own counsel of cautious expediency, he girded to battle for moral principle.

Combat was far from his mind as he nursed campaign wounds at Oyster Bay after the 1910 rout. He conceded that tactically he might have done better "only to have spoken three or four times," but not "without being a craven and shirking my plain duty." Despite blame from either side, he thought that "if I had come out more strongly for Taft, or less strongly, the disaster would have been even greater." The "one comfort" in the defeat in New York was that it prevented "my having to face the very unpleasant task of deciding whether or not to accept the nomination in 1912." Instead, he and Edith could happily relax "out here in our own home, with our books and pictures and bronzes, and big wood fires, and horses to ride, and the knowledge that our children are doing well." He had earned his rest; he was "perfectly willing to step aside and see younger, or at least newer and more vigorous, men take up the task."

Robert M. La Follette was not slow to do so. With Senator Jonathan Bourne of Oregon he issued a manifesto that led in January 1911 to formation of a National Progressive Republican League dedicated to various democratic reforms, including popular election of senators, direct primaries for state offices, and establishment of the initiative, referendum, and recall. Gifford Pinchot and William Allen White were among the League's charter members, but Roosevelt warily declined to do more than endorse the group's objectives, with certain reservations, in a signed article in *Outlook*. He really doubted the wisdom of the initiative and recall. He was also "very anxious not to appear as going into a movement for the political control of the party," particularly when the League was obviously intended to promote La Follette's presidential candidacy.

On the other hand Roosevelt mended some fences with Taft. He read over the annual message in advance, recording only "agreement and commendation." He offered suggestions on policy toward Japan, and supported the administration's efforts to lower tariffs through a reciprocity agreement with Canada. "Poor Taft!" seemed again and again to fail as a leader, yet Roosevelt was reconciled to simply waiting out the nation's judgment in 1912.

To remain on good terms with all was difficult when Taft's belated effort at tariff reduction by the reciprocity agreement further antagonized the midwestern insurgents. Roosevelt praised that proposal initially because "I firmly believe in Free Trade with Canada for both economic and political reasons." But soon he was admitting that the agrarians had good reason to be dissatisfied; it was "a misfortune that the first movement to lower the duties should . . . benefit our manufacturers while letting the farmers and fishermen pay the necessary *quid pro quo* to Canada." Though he continued privately to support the agreement because it would remove another source of friction with Canada and Great Britain, his advocacy grew faint.

Indeed, it was impossible to remain above the party strife. When it was reported in June 1911 that he had notified the White House that he favored Taft's renomination, Roosevelt at once issued a flat denial: he was not a candidate for 1912 himself and would not support any other man for the nomination. But that statement possibly gave La Follette the final encouragement to declare his own candidacy a fortnight later, which in turn fed Taft's suspicions that Roosevelt was really backing the Wisconsin leader's bid. That was not so, despite La Follette's later allegations to the contrary, but the Taft-

Roosevelt *rapprochement* abruptly ended. After mid-June not a letter passed between them.

Inevitably differences over issues contributed to the estrangement. For beginning in the spring of 1911 Roosevelt sharply disagreed with administration stands on several vital matters. What was more, he expressed himself forcefully in *Outlook*, for which he was serving as contributing editor to "bring in some money" and because the work and association were "most congenial to me." It did little good to forswear much speechmaking, as he did in June to keep "as much aloof from politics as possible," if Taft and everyone else could read his critical comments in a national magazine.

The arbitration treaties negotiated with Great Britain and France furnished one major point of attack. Designed as prototypes for bilateral pacts with other countries which would agree to submit "justiciable" disputes to arbitration, they represented Taft's fondest hope for a legal alternative to war. But Roosevelt's bellicose nationalism erupted at the possibility of arbitrating matters of such vital interest as honor and independence. Decrying the "maudlin sentiment" for the treaties among "mushy philanthropists" in the growing peace movement, he took the lead in opposition outside the Senate until the administration in March 1912 bowed in defeat. On no other issue did his ultimate reliance upon power so clearly clash with Taft's higher devotion to law.

The President's release of 12,800 acres of public lands for private port facilities on Controller Bay, the only remaining outlet from the Bering coal fields in Alaska, also drew Roosevelt's fire in *Outlook* that summer of 1911. But no executive action affected him more personally than the Justice Department's filing of a suit under the Sherman Act, in October 1911, against United States Steel. For unbeknownst to Taft, though not to his Attorney General, the government's case included the charge that acquisition of Tennessee Coal and Iron during the Panic of 1907 had abetted the Steel Corporation's monopoly. Since Roosevelt as President had not objected to that stock purchase — for reasons to which he had just testified before a committee of Congress in August — the conclusion was obvious: either he had been deceived, as the government's petition specifically claimed, or he had aided in creating a more gigantic trust. It was equally obvious that in approving the steel suit without checking the bill of particulars, Taft at the very least had committed a major blunder.

Furious with Taft and the Attorney General for "playing small, mean and foolish politics in this matter," Roosevelt published a spirited reply in *Outlook* in November 1911. He again denied that he had been misled as to the motives of Gary and Frick in coming to him in 1907, or by the facts they had presented; their company had not increased its share of the nation's steel production by more than two per cent through the acquisition, and by 1910 controlled only 54.3 per cent of total output compared to 58 per cent in 1906. He then attacked the administration's "hopeless" attempt to meet the trust problem through "a succession of lawsuits" under the Sherman Act; it was impractical and unwise "to put the business of the country back into the middle of the eighteenth century." What the times demanded was a great increase in federal regulatory power over industry, vested in an independent agency similar to the Interstate Commerce Commission. Under such supervision, he concluded, he would even permit the setting of industrial prices.

Not until 1920 would the Supreme Court finally rule against the government in the U. S. Steel case, but Roosevelt's slashing assault stirred immediate and widespread interest. Indeed, the article "caused what evidently had been a very strong undercurrent to come to the surface," he wrote a month later, "in the shape of talk about my nomination for the Presidency." Before the steel suit, he had opposed or discounted such talk; he had continued to "hope we can carry Taft through." When the Progressive League endorsed La Follette in mid-October, moreover, Roosevelt had continued "to expect every friend of mine to do everything in his power to prevent any movement looking toward my nomination." But on October 27, 1911, the day the charges against U. S. Steel appeared, he had given Governor Hiram Johnson of California the first definite sign of yielding to appeals to run. As that pressure had mounted swiftly after the trust article appeared, he had given like signs to Jim Garfield and other Ohioans already booming "Roosevelt for President."

Utterly disillusioned about Taft, and critical of La Follette chiefly for failing to denounce socialists and labor extremists as fearlessly as he did plutocrats, Roosevelt in December began in earnest to explore his own chances at the G.O.P. nomination. For he believed that he was the only man who could possibly defeat Taft. And though for many reasons "it would be from my standpoint a very great misfortune to be nominated," Roosevelt informed political friends, he could not shirk his duty if "the bulk of the people wanted a given job done, and for their own sakes, and not mine, wanted me to do that job." In theory he would sit back to await the people's call. In effect he invited his close supporters to reveal the extent of the popular demand.

Roosevelt's motives were such a mixture of resentment against Taft and ambition for himself, of devotion to progressive government and response to public acclaim, that not even he could fully understand them. Nor could he accurately appraise the proportions of the drive that early in 1912 gathered such strength to induce him to run. But by mid-January the disabilities produced by uncertainty as to his intent began to outweigh any personal advantage in delaying a decision. So Roosevelt took the further step of indicating to publisher Frank Munsey a hesitancy to speak without "some tangible evidence" of "a real popular movement" that expressed "a demand from at least a substantial portion of the plain people."

Widely circulated through the burgeoning Roosevelt organization, the Munsey letter sparked the hasty assembling of "some tangible evidence" — a round-robin letter of February 10, signed by seven Republican governors and endorsed by several more, affirming their con-

viction that "a large majority" of Republican voters and
of the people favored his nomination and election. La
Follette's tragic breakdown during a speech at Philadelphia had meantime furnished Gifford Pinchot and other
Roosevelt men in the Progressive League a convenient
excuse for switching allegiance publicly. While still
doubtful whether he could beat out Taft, Roosevelt was
at last convinced that "the sentiment among the people is two or three to one in my favor." There was no
use in debating further. On February 24 he notified the
governors that he would "accept the nomination for
President if it is tendered to me."

A consummate politician, Roosevelt rightly feared that
he could not muster the power to prevail. The effort
could be adequately financed by George W. Perkins,
the Pinchots, and other wealthy individuals, but the Roosevelt organization across the country was hastily constructed and comparatively inexperienced. The effort
could be successfully made to win delegates in states
that had preferential primaries, but elsewhere and especially in the "rotten boroughs" of the South, the administration firmly held the advantage. And though the
President could be soundly criticized, the countercharges
of faithlessness to Taft, to La Follette, to the "third-term
tradition" itself, would weigh heavily in the balance.

But in this crisis Roosevelt subordinated an expedient
concern for his own power to a moral devotion to principle. He indicated as much in setting forth his "platform" before the Ohio Constitutional Convention on
February 21, by coming out boldly for recall of judicial

decisions involving constitutional interpretation on the state level. To his mind this step would avoid the extremes of recall of judges (as ultra-progressives proposed) and inaction upon unpopular decisions that frustrated social and economic reform (as ultra-conservatives demanded). It would conform to his more general aim to champion a "middle way" between the "Robespierre type" and the "Bourbon type." But from many letters and discussions over the past year, and from the reaction to his October speech criticizing the New York Court of Appeals for its labor verdicts, Roosevelt well knew how strongly many moderate Republicans resisted any democratic tampering with the judiciary.

He braved the certain storm of protest and misrepresentation because for thirty years the courts had been the great obstacle to "measures for social and industrial betterment which every other civilized nation takes as a matter of course." He braved it because "wealth should be the servant, not the master, of the people." He thus dramatized anew, as he had at Osawatomie, his basic difference with William Howard Taft. For Taft's supreme allegiance was to the law, his prime concern as President had been to put reforms into "legal execution." Roosevelt's greater allegiance was to justice; his main concern as President and after had been to employ federal power to meet the people's just demands.

If the party machinery had been more responsive to the public will, Roosevelt could have captured the 1912 nomination. For where voters were permitted to express their preference in primaries, or where the conventions were relatively free, delegates pledged to him usually won a majority. Indeed, where Roosevelt Republicans were able to introduce the direct primary in 1912 — Illinois, Maryland, Massachusetts, Ohio, Pennsylvania, and South Dakota — he carried the elections in all except Massachusetts, which he split with Taft. In the six other primary races Roosevelt lost only North Dakota (to La Follette, who also took Wisconsin uncontested) and New Hampshire (to Taft).

But in most states the traditional convention system still ruled. And though the Roosevelt forces there took Maine, Kansas, and Oklahoma, generally the battle turned against them. Their charges of "fraudulent and unlawful acts" in district conventions in Indiana and Michigan were of no avail. Nor could they keep the state conclaves in Colorado and Washington from ignoring some county results to send solid Taft delegations to Chicago. With the conservative press in full cry against the "revolutionary" schemes of that "madman" Roosevelt, the Taft regulars fought none too scrupulously. Hardened professionals among the rebels replied in kind. This was politics, but not even in 1884 had the Republicans been so sharply divided.

La Follette continued in the campaign to attack both his opponents; Roosevelt and Taft saved their sharpest barbs for each other. Stung by Roosevelt's criticism of the administration, and convinced that "I represent a safer and saner view of our government and its Constitution," the President entered the fray in April by charging that on all counts Roosevelt was not giving him "a square deal." At the same time the executive branch released evidence intended to show that Roosevelt in 1907 had not pressed antitrust action against George W. Perkins' International Harvester. Charges flew back and forth as the debate descended into personal invective. "I am a man of peace, and I don't want to fight," Taft declared. "But when I do fight I want to hit hard," he added; "Even a rat in a corner will fight."

As the national convention drew near it became apparent that control there would turn on the 252 seats the Roosevelt side was contesting. About 100 of these were legitimate challenges, of which Roosevelt needed to win only 70 to gain the nomination. But the administration dominated the National Republican Committee which would rule on all disputes. "My own belief is that I shall probably not be nominated at Chicago," Roosevelt wrote a British editor on June 4, "but they will have to steal the delegates outright in order to prevent my nomination, and if the stealing is flagrant no one can tell what the result will be."

As early as mid-April, in replying to Michigan Governor Osborn's suggestion of forming a new party, Roosevelt had conceded that "we will have to consider it" if "political thugs" exploited the convention system to nominate Taft "against the will of the States where the people are really represented." And when the National Committee began on June 7 to resolve one contest after another in Taft's favor, to a total of 238 out of 252, the last bonds of Roosevelt's party loyalty snapped. Rushed to Chicago too late to influence the situation, he told his supporters assembled on the convention's eve that he would not be bound by its proceedings unless seventy-six of the decisions on contested seats were overruled. He stuck to that demand while the Taft forces elected Elihu Root permanent chairman over Roosevelt's candidate, 558 to 502, and the credentials committee commenced to confirm the National Committee's findings. Within that convention Roosevelt's cause was clearly lost.

At a conference of progressive leaders the evening of the second day, June 20, the sentiment for a party bolt was strong enough to insure a respectable showing. Later that night Frank Munsey and George W. Perkins assured the venture of financial support: "Colonel, we will see you through." The next afternoon Roosevelt revealed that a new national nominating convention was likely, and on the final morning he requested his supporters not to vote at all in "this successful fraud." Thereupon 343 delegates sat silent as Taft was duly renominated with 561 votes to 107 for Roosevelt and 41 for La Follette.

Compromise had ever been Roosevelt's forte, but by June 1912 the G.O.P. split over principles and personalities had become too wide to be bridged. Rather than cooperate with Roosevelt, La Follette preferred to see Taft nominated, whereas Roosevelt was adamantly opposed to any other candidate than himself. And once this "fraudulent" convention had spoken, Roosevelt saw no honorable course but to disown the verdict. More than that, he believed that he could lead the bulk of the

Republicans into a new organization of the old party. A clear majority of them had supported his pre-convention fight against intrenched privilege. Most of them would rally to the same fight, so his closest advisers assured him, in the national campaign. If the Democrats named a conservative candidate, the new Progressive Party would stand a good chance of coming out on top.

But even if the Democrats chose a progressive, Roosevelt was committed by his pledge to a near-hysterical gathering of his delegates at Chicago, the evening after adjournment, to accept the nomination of a new national convention regularly called and regularly elected. Convinced that he had been "robbed" not "steamrollered," that he could not let down his supporters, that the cause he championed was more important than his personal fate, Roosevelt made the break that many of the governors and politicians who had backed him could not. He persisted though the Democrats early in July nominated the progressive Governor Woodrow Wilson of New Jersey. Conceding privately that victory was now "a forlorn hope," Roosevelt would not retire as Brooks Adams counselled, nor go over to Wilson's support as La Follette did — the Democrats were still the distrusted opposition, the Progressives were the only soldiers worthy of leadership. If he expected to lead them ever again, he had to command them in this critical hour.

A militant, evangelistic mood dominated the ten thousand and more who thronged on August 5 into the same Chicago Auditorium where Roosevelt seven weeks before had summoned his followers to combat for the Republican nomination. Comparatively young and inexperienced in politics, most delegates to the Progressive National Convention were earnest, middle-class citizens who broke frequently into "Onward, Christian Soldiers" and "The Battle Hymn of the Republic." They thrilled to Beveridge's impassioned keynote address ("We stand for a nobler America . . . we enlist for the war") and to Roosevelt's dramatic "Confession of Faith" in political and economic reform ("Our cause is based on the eternal principles of righteousness. . . . We stand at Armageddon, and we battle for the Lord"). They nominated California Governor Hiram Johnson as Roosevelt's running mate upon a platform distinguished by the most advanced social thought of the times.

Had Roosevelt been the Republican candidate he could not have endorsed unemployment insurance and old-age pensions, woman suffrage, and the other radical proposals that inspired progressives then and later. But he had to muffle his jingoistic nationalism around Jane Addams and the other peace advocates, and his stand on trusts aroused the greatest dissension in reform ranks. Antitrust spokesmen devoted to the old competitive ideal wanted to strengthen the Sherman Act through prohibitions on specific business practices. But Roosevelt sided with George W. Perkins in opposing a plank to this effect, with the result that the platform finally omitted all mention of the Sherman Act, in favor of a demand for a new federal commission with wide regulatory power over interstate industry.

Suspicion about Perkins' reform credentials bedeviled the subsequent campaign, for over strong protests he was elected chairman of the Progressive Executive Committee. And the antitrust issue continued to rankle, for Woodrow Wilson espoused a program similar to the one Perkins so vehemently opposed. But the new party would have sorely missed the industrialist's hard work in the cause to which he contributed so much time and money. Roosevelt appreciated such efforts, and was more than willing to make trust regulation the leading issue of the campaign. Despite criticism without and within his party, he championed federal executive supervision of corporations under a broad mandate, against Wilson's judicial restraint under specific law.

As Wilson warmed to the campaign under Louis Brandeis' tutelage, however, the difference between "regulated monopoly" under the New Nationalism and "regulated competition" under the New Freedom became more obscure. At the same time Wilson began to speak of economic justice and social righteousness in a general way that softened his earlier criticisms of the Progressive platform. Though Roosevelt's was a more coherent philosophy, that Wilson himself would carry out as President (as in the Federal Trade Commission), progressive Democrats for the most part stayed within the regular party.

Roosevelt's indignation at the "theft" of the nomination had its most serious consequence where the Progressives wanted to cooperate with the Republicans in running candidates for state and national offices other than the presidential electors. In a decision as moral as it was politically disastrous, Roosevelt rejected any compromise here; he insisted that unless he had the support of every Republican on a state ticket, the Progressives had to run a third slate. In only six states, in which the Progressives controlled the organization, was it possible to fashion a mutually satisfactory list of candidates; almost everywhere else there had to be two tickets. As a result, few incumbents seeking re-election courted loss of their own power by joining the new party, and Roosevelt's chances were greatly diminished.

Caught up in a militant crusade that forsook expediency, the Colonel did not let a would-be assassin's bullet at Milwaukee in October keep him from winding up the campaign on a vigorous note. At the polls he vindicated his cause within the party by compiling 4,126,020 votes to Taft's 3,483,922, for eighty-eight electors to Taft's eight. But the Republican split elected Wilson with 6,286,124 popular (forty-five per cent of the total) and 435 electoral votes. The Democrats won both houses of Congress and many governorships. The Progressives garnered but a few congressional seats and one governorship. "We had all the money, all the newspapers and all the political machinery against us," Roosevelt concluded with some accuracy, "and, above all, we had the habit of thought of the immense mass of dull unimaginative men who simply vote according to the party symbol." That was some comfort for a soldier who had battled for the Lord.

VIII

"Even Peace Second to Righteousness"

1913-1919

HIS CRUSADING ARDOR spent, the Colonel recognized political reality. The Progressive Party had actually fulfilled its high purpose by forcing the Democrats to cope with the vital issues; in Wilson's victory, the Progressive movement had really scored a triumph. But the new party had not supplanted the old as the Republicans had risen out of the Whigs and antislavery Democrats in 1856 — an historical parallel Roosevelt had hoped to repeat in 1912. And since the G.O.P. leaders at Chicago had "perfected their organization so as to render it certain that they could cheat us just as readily four years hence" — a factor that he admitted in November had figured in his personal decision to launch the new party — the prospect for the Progressives in 1916 was indeed bleak.

Yet a leader who had polled four million votes and commanded a nationwide organization could not alter direction quickly. Moreover, there was the chance that Wilson could not avoid a break among the Democrats.

Roosevelt therefore concentrated upon preserving unity within Progressive ranks. He mollified the radicals by accepting the Sherman Act provision which had been stricken from the antitrust plank at Chicago. On the other hand he insisted that the party needed George W. Perkins, and politicians like William Flinn of Pennsylvania, if it was to be at all effective. "We have no excuse for existing excepting as the radical party," he wrote Amos Pinchot, an outspoken foe of Perkins, "but I want to keep it as the party of sane and tempered radicalism such as that of Abraham Lincoln."

The Lincoln image was one that Roosevelt had invoked ever more frequently since 1906. But in November 1912, he saw that unlike the Republicans in 1856 after their defeat, the Progressives did not have "the clear-cut issues as to which we can take one side and our opponents the other side, and as to which the conscience of the people is deeply stirred." And while he assured Minnesota Progressives that "there shall be no retreat from the position we have taken," he was deeply pessimistic about his own future. He did not think he could ever decide "to repeat the experiment," he said privately, and the "endless fussing" to keep the Progressives together was "very weary work" suited "for an ambitious young colonel, and not for a retired major general."

The work grew wearier as multimillionaire Frank Munsey deserted in February 1913 to advocate amalgamation of the Progressives with the Republicans. Unable to mend old ties so quickly, Roosevelt looked to the past mainly for justification. He eloquently defended his kind of history in the presidential address ("History as Literature") before the American Historical Association. He composed an autobiography through 1908 that made a moving apologia for the New Nationalism. He easily won a libel suit against a Michigan editor who had repeated all the campaign slander that "Roosevelt lies and curses in a most disgusting way; he gets drunk too, and that not infrequently." Finally he sailed south in October to explore the primitive wilds of Paraguay and Brazil.

Had Roosevelt died of infection and fever on the Amazon, as he came near doing, he would have attained a kind of martyrdom in the progressive cause for which he had taken such a hammering. He would have avoided some trying passages that marred the closing years of his career. But his sturdy physique saw him through the jungle ordeal. It left him well enough to discharge remaining debts to the Progressive party in the congressional elections of 1914. It gave him strength for the last great cause to which he dedicated himself, the defeat of Imperial Germany.

A FAR SMALLER CROWD than had greeted his 1910 homecoming portended worse troubles within Progressive ranks that spring of 1914. Beveridge and William Allen White represented a radical and mainly western sentiment still adamantly opposed to the steps others were urging toward cooperation with the Republicans. Much the same sentiment backed Amos Pinchot in his attack upon George Perkins for "big business" attitudes expressed in the *Progressive Bulletin.* "Ours is a party of great enthusiasm and great independence," Roosevelt had written the young curmudgeon, Harold L. Ickes, "and therefore with much less cohesion than the old parties." But Pinchot's letter to the National Committee in May 1914, advocating that Perkins resign, seemed to threaten immediate dissolution.

Roosevelt promptly quelled the revolt by indicating that if Perkins was forced out he would leave also. At the same time he sided with Perkins in a major speech at Pittsburgh, criticizing the Clayton antitrust measure that the Wilson administration had promoted (but soon neglected in favor of the more Rooseveltian Federal Trade Commission bill), and blaming the decline in business activity on the lowering of protective duties by the Democrats in the Underwood tariff. In fact, Roosevelt manifested a greater desire to defeat the Democrats than to continue to war with Republicans. To the disgust of radical Progressives who wanted to maintain a permanent and separate organization across the nation, he contended that the party in New York ought to nominate an independent Republican for governor.

Roosevelt's gubernatorial scheme showed how far he had adjusted to political reality. The Progressives in New York, as in most states, had no chance of attaining power if they maintained a "purist" stand toward party labels. By stressing the democratic principles they shared with independents in the old parties, however, and by cooperating on that basis, the Progressives might wield a preponderant influence against the machine bosses. What he sought in New York was some kind of a joint ticket that would undermine the regular organizations without compromising reform ideals. But naturally he was attacked from either side for advocating "fusion," with the result that his candidate refused finally to run except as a Republican in company with fellow Republicans.

Roosevelt's forthright condemnation of the corrupt alliance of the New York machines prompted Republican boss William A. Barnes to file a libel suit that Roosevelt eventually won. But the failure of his gubernatorial gambit left "but one course for me to follow this Fall consistently with retaining my own self-respect and acting as I deem my honorable obligations require," he decided in August 1914, "and that is to fight straight-out for the Progressive party in Illinois, in New York, in Kansas and in Louisiana, all alike." Heavy of heart at the futility of the effort, he steeled himself to a speaking schedule as strenuous as he had ever undertaken. "I have done everything this fall that everybody has wanted," he remarked to a newsman at its conclusion. "This election makes me an absolutely free man."

As Roosevelt had foreseen, the straight-out campaign ended in disaster. Of the able leaders who sought major offices, like Beveridge and Garfield and Gifford Pinchot, only Hiram Johnson won, and his re-election as governor showed Roosevelt that California was "in favor of Progressivism with a small 'p'." Many Old Guard Republicans swept out in 1912 were returned to Congress, where the Democratic majority in the House was reduced from seventy-three to twenty-five. "East of Indiana there is no state in which the Progressive party remains in condition even to affect the balance of power between the two old parties," Roosevelt observed. "As for the Republican party, at the moment the dog has returned to its vomit."

Contrary to Amos Pinchot's explanation that the Progressives had not been radical enough, the election proved to Roosevelt that they had been too radical. The prime issue had been the business recession, for "if men have not enough to eat, they are entirely uninterested in social justice; they want a job." The nation had voted Republican as the only way "to rebuke the administration and . . . to do anything possible toward securing a return of prosperity." If the Progressives had followed his initial tactic in New York, and had emphasized "the economic side of our program that told for prosperity," they might have survived the conservative reaction better. But "the fundamental trouble" was that after twelve years of agitation and accomplishment, "the country was sick and tired of reform."

Aside from Hiram Johnson, Roosevelt gloomily decided, "the people as a whole have had enough of all reformers and especially of me." The Progressives ought to keep their organization together, but permit "a very wide latitude for action in different states" toward cooperation with "Progressive-Republicans." Instead of launching a fresh drive for the 1912 platform, the new party ought for the present to follow a policy of "silence and sit tight." And for a year or more he himself ought to "avoid political speech-making or any appearance of taking active part in the party politics of the day."

Roosevelt was too much the politician to despair long that he was finished as a party leader. But if he was ready to be more expedient on the domestic issues of reform that had inspired the Bull Moosers, he could not do so upon American policy toward the great war that broke out over Europe in August 1914. The defeat of Imperial Germany became for him another crusade that subordinated personal considerations. It became a last cause that brought out the worst with the best in his intensely combative nature.

The mere fact that Wilson was a Democrat aroused partisanship, but as early as September 1913 Roosevelt had again struck up correspondence with Henry Cabot Lodge to condemn the administration's Mexican policy. Roosevelt's opinion of Wilson ("a ridiculous creature in international matters") and William Jennings Bryan ("the most contemptible figure we have ever had as Secretary of State") had only worsened at their proposed "cooling-off" treaties of conciliation, and especially at their negotiation with Colombia providing that the United States apologize for her part in the Panama revolution of 1903 and pay a $25,000,000 indemnity. Such an abject concession would not get through the Senate while Roosevelt lived, but by the summer of 1914 he disliked Wilson as much as he had ever resented Taft.

As the guns of August brought Wilson's proclamation of neutrality and Germany's swift invasion of France through Belgium, Roosevelt stilled his protest. He was not sure initially, remembering his own repugnance at words without action, what he would have done as President. He thought the conflict had been inevitable, the need for withholding immediate judgments imperative. And he remained silent publicly because he had promised the Progressive leaders not to attack Wilson's foreign policy during the fall campaign. But by late September he had determined that Belgium had been wronged, by October he was writing privately that had he been President he would have interfered as a signatory of the Hague Treaties to preserve Belgian neutrality.

By its violation of a solemn obligation to Belgium, Germany in Roosevelt's view posed a threat to international order that other world powers ought to oppose in concert. More than that, he envisaged a threat to the Panama Canal and the Western Hemisphere if Germany destroyed the British Empire. But "if I should advocate all that I myself believe," he wrote Rudyard Kipling in November 1914, "I would do no good among our people, because they would not follow me." Seemingly protected by the wide Atlantic, "our people believe that they have nothing to fear from the present contest, and that they have no responsibility concerning it." If Roosevelt was to rouse them to action, it could not be by appeals to American security. It would have to be in defense of American neutral rights.

The precept of "the just man armed" still guided Roosevelt, but his bias against Germany directed his sense of justice against the neutral course of the administration.

His reliance upon armed strength turned him into a slashing opponent of a President who neglected preparedness in favor of diplomatic notes. Without the restraints imposed by high office, Roosevelt became a violent partisan; he never tried to understand Wilson's patient search for peace through negotiation. Indeed, the Warrior became so infuriated with the Priest as to lose all sense of proportion, until his closing speech of the 1916 campaign even summoned up "from the ooze of the ocean bottom and from graves in foreign lands . . . the shadows of the helpless whom Mr. Wilson did not dare protect lest he might have to face danger."

An apostle who "always put even peace second to righteousness," Roosevelt moved to the forefront of the forces that pressed a reluctant executive toward preparedness and eventually war. He became "the bugle that woke America," but at the cost of whatever chance he might have had at the Republican nomination in 1916. The G.O.P. leaders did not want him anyway, but particularly not after he carried his militant nationalism into the German-American strongholds of the isolationist Midwest on a speech-making tour in May 1916. The bosses accepted his earlier statement that "it would be a mistake to nominate me unless the country has in its mood something of the heroic." They prepared to nominate the austere, non-controversial Supreme Court Justice respected by the German-Americans, Charles Evans Hughes.

The Progressives still wanted Roosevelt to run, but he refused to let them use his candidacy to influence the Republican convention against Hughes. Roosevelt finally showed how far he had pushed domestic issues to the background by insisting that Perkins present the name of Henry Cabot Lodge to the Bull Moosers assembled at Chicago at the same time as the Republicans. To the veterans of 1912 this suggestion was so fantastic as to be insulting; they howled down Perkins and angrily nominated Roosevelt. But he declined their offer if Hughes explained his position on "the vital issues of the day" to the satisfaction of the Progressive National Committee.

Some Progressives never forgave Roosevelt for the way he had maneuvered them back into the Republican party. Yet even Amos Pinchot later recognized that in commending Lodge as an economic reformer, Roosevelt had really selected the Republican who most closely shared his views on foreign policy. By the same logic, he at last supported Hughes because the G.O.P. nominee was the only hope for displacing "He kept us out of war" Wilson. Democratic propagandists appreciated that reasoning. "Wilson and Peace with Honor?" they queried, "or Hughes with Roosevelt and War?"

Wilson won the electoral battle by the narrowest of margins, but in April 1917 he at last admitted defeat in his struggle to resolve the crisis without a call to arms. In Wilson's words, "the right is more precious than the peace," Roosevelt found vindication for his own campaign. Through the years of neutrality the President had better represented the wishes of the majority of Americans, but war's coming restored and even enhanced Roosevelt's popularity. After wandering in the wilderness, it was good to be back in the affections of the people.

For the heroic boy in Roosevelt it was 1898 all over again, but no amount of pressure could persuade the Commander in Chief to entrust him with command of a volunteer division. His dreams of romantic glory frustrated, he participated vicariously through four sons in service. His body often pained by fever and abscesses, he buttressed the home front through countless articles and speeches extolling a united effort. His theme of "one hundred per cent" loyalty translated into condemnation of pacifists and socialists, but his running fire of criticism of Wilson's war leadership was constructive.

By 1918 Roosevelt was widely regarded as the foremost contender for the next Republican nomination. If the people wanted him, he was willing to take it, but he did not intend to submit to reaction. In March at the Maine Republican convention he rekindled old progressive fires by charting the path of moderate reform that the nation would have to follow in the postwar world. "I think I do not overstate the matter," he informed William Allen White afterwards, "when I say that the Maine Progressives felt that my speech and its reception amounted to the acceptance, by the Republicans of Maine, of the Progressive platform of 1912 developed and brought up to date."

More than likely Roosevelt would have failed to make the G.O.P. "the party of sane, constructive radicalism, just as it was under Lincoln." More than likely he would have compromised principles too much if he had ever tried. But it was the misfortune of the nation and the party that he was not to have that chance. He could have kept the Republicans from so far succumbing to domestic reaction in the 1920's. And though he would have been as obstructive as Lodge toward the Versailles settlement, he could have helped America avoid the worst follies of peace without power.

In the summer of 1918 his store of energy for such efforts was giving out. He had been hospitalized for a month in February; in July the news of his youngest son's death, in a plane crash behind enemy lines, shook him grievously. Immensely proud that his boys had wanted to be in the thick of the fighting, he found solace in the thought that Quentin had been a hero — "He had his crowded hour of glorious triumph." Yet the loss killed the boy in Theodore Roosevelt. "It is a very sad thing to see the young die," he wrote Georges Clemenceau, "when the old who are doing nothing, as I am doing nothing, are left alive."

By sheer will he contributed his bit to the Republican victory in the fall elections, but the day of the Armistice found him again in the hospital suffering from inflammatory rheumatism. By Christmas Day he was well enough to return to Oyster Bay. "I wonder if you will ever know how I love Sagamore Hill," he remarked to Edith as he rested in the bedroom overlooking Long Island Sound on Sunday, January 5, 1919. Early the next morning he died in his sleep.

Among the mourners at the funeral was William Howard Taft, with whom Roosevelt happily had been reconciled for some months. But there was no eulogy, nor could any man have encompassed what Theodore Roosevelt had meant to family, to friends, to all who had ever known him. With amazing versatility he had packed three or four careers into sixty short years. With enormous zest for life he had enriched a whole generation. With abiding love of country he had wielded power as he saw the people's interest. Great or near great, he had dominated an era in American life.

A Note on the Sources

THIS BIOGRAPHY does not owe much to the early, often adulatory, studies such as William R. Thayer, *Theodore Roosevelt* (Boston, 1919) or J. B. Bishop, *Theodore Roosevelt and His Times* (2 volumes, New York, 1920). Nor does it reflect the debunking attitude that swiftly succeeded in the spritely, ever-popular narrative of Henry F. Pringle, *Theodore Roosevelt: A Biography* (New York, 1931). Rather it takes its inspiration from the more realistic mood of the power-conscious post-World War Two era, first evidenced in George E. Mowry, *Theodore Roosevelt and the Progressive Movement* (Madison, 1946) and more especially Elting E. Morison and John M. Blum, eds., *The Letters of Theodore Roosevelt* (8 volumes, Cambridge, 1951-54). My own investigation of Roosevelt's governorship reached the dissertation stage in 1950; much revised, it was later published as *Governor Theodore Roosevelt: The Albany Apprenticeship, 1898-1900* (Cambridge, 1965).

For primary sources beyond my own basic research on the period before 1900, I have relied heavily upon *The Letters* so ably selected by Elting Morison and John Blum from Roosevelt's voluminous correspondence. In addition, I have consulted the Roosevelt House Papers and the capacious Roosevelt Scrapbooks in the Theodore Roosevelt Memorial Association Collection in the Harvard College Library, as well as Hermann Hagedorn, ed., *The Works of Theodore Roosevelt* (20 volumes, National Edition, New York, 1926) and Henry Cabot Lodge, ed., *Selections from the Correspondence of Theodore Roosevelt and Henry Cabot Lodge, 1884-1918* (2 volumes, New York, 1925).

I am further indebted to the editors of *The Letters* for their copious and perceptive footnotes, their chronologies, and the illuminating essays in the appendices. Parts of the articles John Blum contributed to *The Letters* later appeared in his brilliant *The Republican Roosevelt* (Cambridge, 1954), which I found especially useful in Chapters IV and VI of this volume, but which in brief compass represents the most thoughtful and stimulating interpretation of the postwar era.

The reassessment produced by publication of *The Letters* and *The Republican Roosevelt* is apparent in the successive treatments of Roosevelt in Richard Hofstadter, *The American Political Tradition and the Men Who Made It* (New York, 1948), *The Age of Reform, From Bryan to F.D.R.* (New York, 1955), and *Anti-Intellectualism in American Life* (New York, 1962). Similarly, in the 1961 paperback edition of his *Men of Good Hope: A Story of American Progressives* (New York, 1951), Daniel Aaron prescribed Blum's study for "a corrective to what I now consider my too biased estimate of Theodore Roosevelt." For a comprehensive analysis of the general shift, see Dewey W. Grantham, Jr., "Theodore

Roosevelt in American Historical Writing, 1945-1960," *Mid-America*, XLIII (1961), 3.

By 1961, Theodore Roosevelt's new stature among American political leaders seemed secure. It was reflected in the best surveys of the period: George E. Mowry, *The Era of Theodore Roosevelt and the Birth of Modern America, 1900-1912* (New York, 1958) and Arthur S. Link, *Woodrow Wilson and the Progressive Era, 1910-1917* (New York, 1954), both in the New American Nation Series. And it distinguished the new study by William H. Harbaugh, *Power and Responsibility: The Life and Times of Theodore Roosevelt* (New York, 1961), which remains the best full-length biography. Harbaugh writes with particular authority of the 1914-17 period, but his judicious assessments and thorough research have assisted me greatly in all areas.

Yet as seen in Ray Ginger, *Age of Excess: The United States from 1877 to 1914* (New York, 1965), the more radical historians of the 1960's continue to be highly critical of Roosevelt's record at home and abroad. In foreign policy they rely upon Howard K. Beale, *Theodore Roosevelt and the Rise of America to World Power* (Baltimore, 1956), a most able study which I used in Chapters IV and V, but which I question on its basic assumptions regarding both the Far East and Great Britain. In domestic policy they utilize Gabriel Kolko, *The Triumph of Conservatism: A Reinterpretation of American History, 1900-1916* (New York, 1963), a well-researched but contentious analysis that oversimplifies and distorts "big business" influence upon federal regulation. Most useful to counter Kolko are Robert H. Wiebe's "Business Disunity and the Progressive Movement, 1901-1914," *Mississippi Valley Historical Review,* XLIV (1958), 664, and *Businessmen and Reform: A Study of the Progressive Movement* (Cambridge, 1962); Arthur M. Johnson's "Theodore Roosevelt and the Bureau of Corporations," *Mississippi Valley Historical Review,* XLV (1959), 571, and "Antitrust Policy in Transition, 1908: Ideal and Reality," *Mississippi Valley Historical Review,* XLVIII (1961), 415; and John Braeman, "The Square Deal in Action: A Case Study in the Growth of the 'National Police Power,'" in J. Braeman, R. H. Bremner, and E. Walters, eds., *Change and Continuity in Twentieth-Century America* (Columbus, 1964).

A complete bibliography of the books I consulted would be out of place here, but among the other volumes which I found especially helpful were the following: Carleton Putnam, *Theodore Roosevelt: The Formative Years, 1858-1886* (New York, 1958) — a convincing interpretation of Roosevelt's early life, based upon exhaustive research; Hermann Hagedorn, *The Roosevelt Family of Sagamore Hill* (New York, 1954) — revealing insights into Roosevelt's personal life; Richard W. Leopold, *Elihu Root and the Conservative Tradition* (Boston, 1954) and Robert E. Osgood, *Ideals and Self-Interest in America's Foreign Relations* (Chicago, 1953) — excellent studies of the development of American foreign policy; John A. Garraty, *Henry Cabot Lodge* (New York, 1953) and *Right-Hand Man: The Life of George*

W. *Perkins* (New York, 1960), M. Nelson McGeary, *Gifford Pinchot: Forester-Politician* (Princeton, 1960), and Elting E. Morison, *Turmoil and Tradition: A Study of the Life and Times of Henry L. Stimson* (Boston, 1960) — all valuable biographies of important figures close to Roosevelt; Ira Kipnis, *The American Socialist Movement, 1897-1912* (New York, 1952) — of value in Chapter VI; Henry F. Pringle, *The Life and Times of William Howard Taft* (2 volumes, New York, 1939) — together with Mowry's *Theodore Roosevelt and the Progressive Movement*, an indispensable source for Chapter VII; Samuel P. Hays, *Conservation and the Gospel of Efficiency: The Progressive Conservation Movement, 1890-1920* (Cambridge, 1959) — a penetrating study that should be compared with J. Leonard Bates, "Fulfilling American Democracy: The Conservation Movement, 1907 to 1921," *Mississippi Valley Historical Review,* XLIV (1957), 29; Herbert Croly, *The Promise of American Life* (New York, 1909) — a most influential analysis; and Arthur S. Link, *Wilson the Diplomatist* (Baltimore, 1957) — a stimulating interpretation by Wilson's foremost biographer.

FOR HIS constant inspiration and careful editing I am especially indebted to Oscar Handlin, a wise counselor and a generous friend. I am grateful also to my colleagues, Alfred W. Lever and William Preston, Jr., who read portions of the manuscript, and to Lois E. Engleman for the preparation of the index. For any errors of fact or interpretation I of course remain solely responsible.

The staff of the Harvard College Library was most helpful and I benefited also from the expert secretarial help of Kathryn Goodwin. Much of the research and writing took place during a sabbatical leave granted by Denison University. And Eleanor Osgood Chessman gave each chapter her own intelligent scrutiny.

G. W. C.

Index